MEAT FREE
MOWGLI

MEAT FREE
MOWGLI

Simple & Delicious Plant-Based Indian Meals

NISHA KATONA

NOURISH

EAT WELL, LIVE WELL

For Ma and Monmon: the growers of this family, God's own gardeners

MEAT FREE MOWGLI
Nisha Katona

First published in the UK and USA in 2023 by
Nourish, an imprint of Watkins Media Limited
Unit 11, Shepperton House, 83–93 Shepperton Road
London N1 3DF

enquiries@nourishbooks.com

Publisher: Fiona Robertson
Project Editor: Emily Preece-Morrison
Head of Design & Art Director: Karen Smith
Production: Uzma Taj
Commissioned Photography: Gareth Morgans
Recipe Development and Testing: Sonali Shah
Additional Food Testing: Andy Mountfield
Food Stylist: Bianca Nice
Prop Stylist: Hannah Wilkinson

A CIP record for this book is available from the
British Library

ISBN: 978-1-84899-411-9 (Hardback)
ISBN: 978-1-84899-413-3 (eBook)

10 9 8 7 6 5 4 3 2 1

Typeset in Futura and Minion Pro
Colour reproduction by XY Digital
Printed in Bosnia and Herzegovina

Publisher's note
While every care has been taken in compiling the recipes for
this book, Watkins Media Limited, or any other persons who
have been involved in working on this publication, cannot
accept responsibility for any errors or omissions, inadvertent
or not, that may be found in the recipes or text, nor for any
problems that may arise as a result of preparing one of these
recipes. If you are pregnant or breastfeeding or have any
special dietary requirements or medical conditions,
it is advisable to consult a medical professional before
following any of the recipes contained in this book.

Notes on the recipes
Unless otherwise stated:
Use medium fruit and vegetables
Use medium (US large) organic or free-range eggs
Use fresh herbs, spices and chillies
Use granulated sugar (Americans can use ordinary granulated
sugar when caster sugar is specified)
Do not mix metric, imperial and US cup measurements:
1 tsp = 5ml 1 tbsp = 15ml 1 cup = 240ml

nourishbooks.com

Contents

WELCOME

Welcome

Raised the daughter of a Hindu Brahmin priest, there was always a fug of disdain in our house for meat eating. My parents were, as were many first generation immigrants, keen horticulturalists who grew spinach, beets, radishes, squashes … and used and cooked every part of them. Stems, flowers, leaves and even the peelings. Hinduism, you see, suggests that the fierce energy used to digest heavy meats should be channelled into philosophy and deep thought, into fathoming how to make the world a better place. In India, eateries will presume you are vegetarian – a minor area of the menu will be labelled "non-veg items", from which one may order with a little blush of shame.

While I am not a vegetarian or vegan, I, like many others, have wholeheartedly embraced the need to eat less meat and more veg, both for my own health and that of the planet. As an Indian chef, this felt like the most natural thing in the world, as our cuisine is so heavily geared toward seasonal vegetable-heavy menus anyway. Indian food is the perfect go-to cuisine for the modern family that wants to eat less meat. And thus, the idea for *Meat Free Mowgli* was born – a collection of simple, plant-based meals in the Mowgli style we know and love.

The Indian meat-free kitchen is one with aeons of heritage. For thousands of years, the average Indian home kitchen has celebrated vegetables with each passing season. While not all religions advocate vegetarianism or veganism, at least a quarter of India's population are strictly vegetarian, so the eating of plant-based dishes is ingrained in our society. This means there are so many wonderful options to choose from that putting together this collection of recipes was a dream. The Indian spices that I love enhance and highlight the naturally wonderful flavours of plants so effortlessly.

When I started planning this book I knew that I wanted the recipes to be as simple and stress-free as possible. Like most people, I need the recipes I cook at home to fit into my busy life and want them to be on the table in as short a time as possible! And the glory of cooking with vegetables is that they are at their best when cooked exactly that way – simply and quickly. With a few basic spices in your arsenal, most vegetables can be cooked in a pan "dry-fry" style, and you have an enormous recipe repertoire at your disposal just like that! Some recipe ideas are a little more time-consuming, requiring a slower cook in a delicious sauce or the careful layering of a biryani, for example, but none are complex.

I also wanted to include a good proportion of vegan dishes. (Again, such a natural thing in Indian cuisine, where in the hot climate, dairy is a treat ingredient rather than an everyday necessity.) With the exception of the Eggs and Dairy chapter, a selection of yogurt-based raitas in various chapters, and a handful of recipes where a slick of butter, the binding quality of an egg or a dash of milk is necessary, I'm pleased to say that the majority of the book is in fact vegan. Where a vegan substitute can be made, I have noted it.

You will find a few Mowgli vegetarian menu classics here, such as the Ruby Wraps (on page 173) and a deconstructed version of my Chat Bombs (Sweet and Sour Chickpea Chaat, on page 90). There are also some clever twists on my Mowgli House favourites: Angry Bird becomes Angry Cauliflower (page 131), Gunpowder Chicken morphs into Gunpowder Florets (page 125), and for a vegetarian take on Mowgli Sticky Wings, you need to check out my Mowgli Sticky Fingers (page 170). There are some new takes on my favourite dals, sides, salads and slaws, and some ideas for accompaniments, from naans to puris to rice dishes. There are plenty of sweets and drinks for good measure, too.

I hope you will enjoy this selection of plant-based recipes. Whether you are a vegetarian or vegan looking for new ideas, or a meat-eater looking for ways to bring more vegetables into your diet, *Meat Free Mowgli* is intended to inspire and spice up your life. Tuck in …

Nisha Katona

Photography: Kat's Films – Katrina Lipska

INTRODUCTION

About This Book

In order to be as useful as possible, I have decided to order the chapters in this book according to the main groups of vegetables. Roots and Alliums; Gourds; Nightshades (an unusual but evocative word for the collection that includes tomatoes, peppers and aubergines/eggplant); Beans, Peas and Lentils; Brassicas and Leafy Greens; and Fruit – all group together quite naturally. Eggs and Dairy warranted a separate chapter to make things easy for vegans trying to navigate the book (although always check each recipe – there may be a small but necessary dash of butter or milk in a handful of recipes). Finally, I have combined those that fitted less easily into one group into a chapter entitled Mushrooms and More!; here you will find sweetcorn, tofu and veggie mince, and some nut- and grain-based recipes.

Find yourself with a glut of potatoes or courgettes/zucchinis? Simply turn to the relevant chapter and discover a collection of fantastic options to try. But don't stop there – the beauty of veg is that they work in endless delicious combinations. You may also find a good recipe featuring potatoes lurking in the Beans, Peas and Lentils chapter, for example, so make good use of the index at the back of the book for a full range of ideas.

And feel free to make the recipes your own. Substitutions are very possible when cooking with vegetables; you can fridge-raid to your heart's content and mix and match in so many combinations. Keep in mind the tried-and-tested formulas (cumin for root vegetables; mustard seed with brassicas; panch phoron and fenugreek with squashes; nigella seed with nightshades) and you can't go wrong. A word of warning: think about the density and water content of your vegetable – don't sub a watery courgette/zucchini for a drier potato without first thinking about the length of time or the way it will need to cook. (A great recipe for using up a surprise veg box selection is Rainbow Chard Chorchuri on page 128.)

Indians will start nearly every meal with vegetable dishes, eaten with flatbreads or rice, before they move on to meat and fish. In the vegetarian Indian kitchen, the meat and fish element is often replaced by dals – lentil and pulse dishes – as they are protein-heavy and rich, so I have provided a good number of these sorts of recipes in this book. You will also find some simple breads you can make yourself without much fuss, as well as some tempting rice dishes to serve alongside.

In the meat-free kitchen, fresh vegetables are the star. In each chapter you will find a number of simple stir-fries – what I call a "dry-fry" – where the flavour of just one vegetable is celebrated. I would often serve a number of these dishes together as part of a sharing feast, so everyone can mix and match to their hearts' content. In addition, you will find plenty of richer, more complex curries with a gravy, perfect for serving with bread or rice.

You will also find some fresh salads and pickles and plenty of chutneys – an essential element of the Indian vegetable kitchen. Seasonal gluts will always be made into chutneys and pickles and these form a vital part of each meal.

I have not ignored those of you with a sweet tooth. There are some tempting desserts, including a tasty chai-time cookie recipe, as well as a few refreshing drinks to complete your meat-free feasts.

What To Do With ...

Vegetables require a lighter touch than the traditional methods of cooking with meat. These ingredients are more delicate and often require little more than frying whole dried spices in hot oil to release the flavours and adding the veg for the required length of time. Then, simply add a little finishing flavour and you are good to go. For saucy curries, or salads, or even dips, pickles or desserts, some plant-based ingredients require more inventive treatment. Here are a few basic notes to bear in mind when approaching the various chapters in this book.

... Roots and Alliums

Potatoes, beets, turnips, carrots: these robust, dense and heavy vegetables can take whatever you want to throw at them. Naturally thickening the dishes in which they are added, they will hold their flavour well and also absorb flavours. Start them off with a zingy headnote spice, such as cumin seeds. Turmeric and chilli can be added partway through cooking. For finishing flavours you could use tomato, ginger, ground coriander and mustard paste. Alliums – onions, shallots and leeks – while often used chopped up and fried as a headnote ingredient, can also be stars in their own right. Try them cooked in larger pieces, or even whole, softened through slow cooking, their flavours tempered and sweetened, and you will find them quite delicious.

... Gourds

Pumpkins, squashes and courgette/zucchini release a lot of water during the cooking process, and so have a tendency to lose flavours if you are not careful. I advocate using robust spicing to ensure they don't become watery disappointments. Strong-flavoured spices, such as mustard seeds, fenugreek seeds and asafoetida/hing, especially when fried together, ensure that punch of flavour is not lost, and you will see them added to a number of the dishes in this chapter. In salads, the freshness of cucumber will similarly benefit from the addition of a bold, fiery flavour, such as ginger.

... Nightshades

Every one of the nightshade family is an essential ingredient in the Indian kitchen. Aubergines/eggplant, capsicums/bell peppers, tomatoes and chillies have a sweet nature and suit the dusty depth of fried nigella seeds as a starting spice. Aubergines work well with white poppy seeds and mustard. India's beloved okra should be fried well before incorporating them into a sauce to eliminate that famous sliminess, or fried until very crisp and used to top soup or rice. Embrace the variety in this enigmatic family of vegetables and stock up on them with abandon, for they have endless uses.

... Beans, Peas and Lentils

I sometimes say that pulses sit in the halfway house between meat and vegetable. Robust and heavy, they bring essential protein and can be treated as you might cook meat. I include chickpeas, kidney beans, green mung lentils, black urad lentils and butter/lima beans in this "heavy" group of pulses. However, split yellow or red lentils that have been stripped of their outer casings are what I consider to be a "light" ingredient. Heavier pulses can be cooked with an onion, garlic and ginger base, powdered spices and a rich and tangy tomato sauce. They can also be finished with yogurt for a velvety finish to the sauce. Light yellow or red lentils are quicker to cook and easier to digest. Cook them with asafoetida/hing, or green chilli to start and fresh coriander to finish. And invest in a pressure cooker if you are going to cook a lot of dal – it will make your life SO much easier. You will also find recipes for fresh green beans, peas and broad/fava beans in this chapter – all versatile, thrifty and popular ingredients in the Indian kitchen.

... Brassicas and Leafy Greens

Start with a headnote spice of mustard seed with a hint of garlic fried in oil, then add your green leafy veg or brassicas and play fast and loose with your finishing flavours. These types of veg can take a lot in terms of flavouring, but treat them gently in the cooking. There is nothing worse than overcooked broccoli or cabbage. Garlic will also work well as a headnote flavour for brassicas. Leafy kale, spinach or chard leaves don't need to be overpowered by onion, but mustard paste and a squeeze of lemon at the end work very well to enhance their natural flavour.

... Fruit

There are so many fantastic options for cooking with fruit in Indian cuisine. The fruits that work best in Indian savoury dishes are those with a bit of sourness to them: lemons, obviously, but also green mangoes and gooseberries. Jackfruit is a fabulous workhorse when it comes to offering a meat-free option for a substantial main, and the sweet-sour nature of apricots is a great foil for earthy ingredients such as kidney beans. Don't miss my mother's recipe for Anuty Mona's Green Mango Chutney (page 149) – it's so good you'll want to eat it with everything.

... Eggs and Dairy

Eggs, cheese, yogurt and milk are highly prized ingredients. In a hot climate, where such ingredients could quickly go off without refrigeration, dishes with dairy are often considered treats or cooked for celebrations. Egg curries are rich and unctuous and treated almost like meat in their preparation, with an onion and garlic base. Paneer is a wonderfully useful ingredient for vegetarians as butter-based paneer curries easily rival their meat-based counterparts. Yogurt is used extensively for its cooling properties, as well as a binding ingredient in marinades, and in fact raitas feature throughout the book depending on their headline ingredient (beetroot/beets and spinach, for example, make great raita flavourings). Desserts too. I've tried to make them a little less sweet than is traditional, partly because I don't have much of a sweet tooth, but also because many Westerners often complain that Indian desserts are too sweet for their palates.

... Mushrooms and Plant-Based Proteins

Mushrooms are a wonderfully versatile ingredient for making plant-based curries. Firmer varieties, such as oyster, chestnut/cremini or shiitake, mimic the properties of meat incredibly well, and make for a substantial and satisfying addition to a saucy dish. They can take the spicing that would normally be used for meaty dishes, so onion, garlic and ginger bases work well with an additional touch of garam masala. I've also included tofu and soya proteins in this chapter, which pair well with traditional meat spicings.

Cooking Tips

Headnote Spices

I have written vast amounts on the concept of Indian spicing, but the basic precept bears repeating. There is a trinity of spices that rules all Indian cooking: turmeric is the "Mother", chilli powder is the "Father" and the third spice is what I call the "headnote" spice, and this will change depending on the type of ingredients being cooked. The headnote spice should be fried in oil first to release its aroma before the main ingredient is added, and it is this third spice that defines the flavour of any dish. It is the perfume-making anchor on which any Indian dish depends.

There are only a handful of headnote spices used in our cuisine: cumin seeds, mustard seeds, nigella seeds, panch phoron, fenugreek, asafoetida/hing, garam masala and curry leaves. I discuss their attributes on page 20. It's worth knowing some of the classic combos. For example, mustard seed pairs well with brassicas, or cumin seed works perfectly with root vegetables.

Finishing Flavours

Indians will cook their dishes to satisfy the six areas of taste on the tongue: salt, sweet, sour, bitter, astringency and pungency. The latter two are particular to Eastern views on the palate; they are largely ignored in the West. But every dish in an Indian kitchen will take these areas of the tongue into account and give them some stimulation.

My armoury of finishing flavours when cooking with vegetables are: tomato, lemon, tamarind, amchur, English mustard paste and garam masala. The first four flavours bring tang and sourness and the final two bring a gentle pungency and punch.

Seasoning

Indian cooks season their dishes with both salt and sugar. It's not unusual to add a little bit of granulated sugar to vegetable dishes in Indian cooking, so you will see this in quite a lot of my recipes. Remember, the tongue needs all its areas of taste to be satisfied for a dish to be successful, so sweet has its place too.

Taste as you go. I cannot stress this enough. Only by tasting can you tweak the amount of salt and sugar in a dish until it reaches that perfect balance. If you have over-salted, simmer a chopped potato in the sauce for a bit – it will absorb some of the excess salt.

It is important to add fresh coriander as a final garnish. Its freshness and verdancy opens the areas of the mouth that taste. In the way that Westerners use lemon or parsley, Indians use coriander leaf to give their dishes the final lift they need. Indians also believe this vital herb cleanses the mouth, giving it carte blanche for enjoying the next flavours to come.

Cooking with Spices

Frying spices in a couple of tablespoons of oil is the secret to unlocking their potential. Only then do they release their aromatic oils to perfume a dish. Ground seed spices are added primarily to meat dishes or to vegetables that are more unyielding or lacklustre, such as potatoes, marrow or pumpkins.

Learning how to fry your spices correctly will enhance your Indian cooking forever. Never cook them for so long that they burn and turn bitter, but make sure that you are cooking them enough. For example, you will know when your cumin seeds are correctly fried when they turn dark brown and go from smelling of tomcat to nutty and fragrant, almost citrussy in aroma. This is the holy grail of Indian cooking, it's the process that cannot be rushed. Get those cumin seeds sizzling to a deep brown in the hot oil before you add any other ingredient to the pan.

Cooking Onions

Another process that should not be rushed. Onions need to be slowly coaxed to a state of soft, golden sweetness in the pan, releasing their natural sugars to caramelize and bring a sweet base note that is essential to most Indian sauce-based dishes.

I have said it before, but I'll say it again: when cooking onions, aim for the colour I would describe as "hotdog brown". The golden brown tangle of onions that you will find on top of a good hotdog is just the right state of cooked that you want your onions to reach before you add other ingredients to an onion-based curry sauce. Cook chopped or sliced onions over a medium-low heat for about 8 minutes and that should do the trick. If you make the mistake of having the heat too high, they will burn, so take your time.

Vegan Dairy Substitutes

The vast majority of recipes in this book are vegan, but there are a few that require yogurt as a base for a sauce or marinade. Likewise, a small dab of butter or ghee, or egg for binding, finds its way into a few recipes. However, vegan dairy substitutes are so versatile these days that you can sub them in quite easily. Here are a few tips:

Where egg is used as a binding agent for a coating that is to be deep-fried, 60ml/¼ cup of aquafaba (the liquid brine drained from a can of chickpeas or other pulses) is an acceptable swap. (I have used panko breadcrumbs for any coatings, as they are vegan.)

Yogurt-based raitas will work just as well when made with coconut yogurt. You will miss none of the creamy tang of the original. Likewise, it will work as a base for a marinade.

Vegan spread can be substituted for butter or ghee, where it is used to cook or fry something. If you are familiar with cooking with vegan spread, you could try swapping it in on the "buttered" curries, but as these recipes have not been tested with this vegan substitute, I cannot vouch for the results.

Plant-based milk can be subbed where dairy milk is used for brushing. Once again, I would caution subbing it directly in the milk-based desserts as they have not all been tested to be vegan. There is a wonderful dairy-free panna cotta on page 215 if you yearn for a creamy dessert.

The Mowgli Spice Box

I don't go in for huge spice lists. Instead, I rely on a tailored list of key spices that bring instant, bold flavour. Each spice in my personalized box has its own distinct flavour and perfume. Learn how to use them, adding them in the right combinations, at the right time, and – importantly – cooking them in the correct way, and they will transform your Indian dishes into complex, flavourful symphonies.

Asian grocery stores and the world food aisle of larger supermarkets often stock spices in large bags and these can be more economical than buying those tiny glass spice jars. But, take care – if you are only going to use spices infrequently, you could be better off buying the smaller amounts. Ground spices will start to go stale after a year of being opened. If you don't think you will get through a whole bag in that time, go small.

If you do buy in bulk, transfer the spices to a jar or airtight container straight after opening them. Don't be too afraid of them going out of date – they just lose their potency and you will need to add a bit more.

Chilli Powder

Chilli powder brings a smoky heat and should be used in moderation. Build it up gradually to get the level of heat you want. I love Kashmiri chilli powder for its intense colour and milder heat.

Panch Phoron

Known as Bengali "five spice", this is an enigmatic combination of cumin, fenugreek, nigella and mustard seeds, and often fennel seeds. It is widely available ready-mixed in Asian grocers or the spice aisle of your supermarket. Typically, we fry this off at the start of making a curry and it brings a nuanced, heady flavour that I adore. For me, this is the ultimate headnote spice for vegetable dishes, so you may find yourself using this a lot in your meat-free kitchen. Take care when frying this mixture off as the seeds can burn quickly, which will make them bitter, so remove them from the heat as soon as they turn golden and add your vegetable to stop them overcooking.

Cumin Seeds

A classic starting spice for vegetable and lentil dishes, these deeply flavourful seeds are often paired with green chilli, especially in Bengali cuisine. Fry them as a headnote spice and those unassuming little seeds transform from bitter pills to become citrussy and almost woody in flavour, and a cornerstone of most curry dishes.

Mustard Seeds

Yellow or black, these are a game changer when cooked with leafy vegetables, and are often paired with a whole dried red chilli. Fry them in hot oil until they start to pop to release their toasty flavour.

Ground Turmeric

This is one of the major building blocks of any curry, providing an earthy base flavour, and I use it a lot. Add it with softer/wetter ingredients to avoid burning it.

Ground Coriander

I find this spice subtle but essential, bringing a delicate, herbal note to curries. I often use it as a finishing note for vegetable dishes.

Ground Cumin

This punchy spice, the ground form of raw cumin seeds, will always bring added oomph to any curry.

Cardamom

I use both the green pods and the smoky black ones. Green cardamom features more in desserts and the meat kitchen. A few black cardamom pods added to the pot when cooking your basmati rice will produce a wonderfully aromatic rice (for the full recipe see my two previous books: *Mowgli Street Food* and *30 Minute Mowgli*).

Garam Masala

Although I call this the ultimate meat spice, there is a definite place for it in vegetarian and vegan cooking. It is a blend of up to 20 different spices and is worth buying in bulk and using frequently. I often add it at the end of cooking a curry as a finishing flavour with more watery ingredients, such as squashes that need a final prod of intensity.

Nigella Seeds

Wonderful when combined with fresh green chillies, these little black seeds should be fried in hot oil at the start of making a dish and bring an earthy hit of flavour.

Black Salt (Kala Namak)

An acquired taste, black salt is actually pink in colour and has a very pungent sulphuric tang. Indians often pair it with fruit or salads, and even use it in cold drinks.

Amchur

Dried green mango powder, this is commonly used as a sharpening tangy flavour, much as we might use lemon or lime in a dish.

Fresh Coriander/Cilantro

Toss chopped coriander through dishes when they are off the heat for a fresh finishing edge. And remember to use both the chopped stems as well as the leaves – they are just as packed with flavour.

Asafoetida/Hing

Asafoetida is also known as hing. It smells pretty dreadful, but magically transforms to lend a buttery aroma to dishes once fried. You will often see it used as a substitute for onion and garlic in Hindu dishes, as it mimics their flavour. Often paired with fenugreek seeds, it is used to start off many vegetable dishes.

1
ROOTS & ALLIUMS

In this chapter, you will find ideas for those essential workhorses of the vegetable world: root veg, including potatoes, beetroot/beets, turnips and carrots, and alliums: onions, shallots, garlic and leeks. Robust and endlessly useful, root veg can take any spicing you want to throw at them. Alliums, meanwhile, don't just have to be chopped up for flavour, they can be stars of the dish in their own right.

IPA Onion Rings

I thought I'd put a twist on onion bhajis for this book and serve you up a recipe for onion rings instead. Beer-battered onion rings are firm fast-food favourites, but add some Indian spicing (and some hoppy India Pale Ale, of course) to the batter and it takes them to another level. Served with Nisha's Quick Indian Ketchup (page 83), they're a great starter for an Indian feast with a difference.

SERVES 4–6

vegetable oil, for deep-frying

75g/2¾oz/¾ cup gram flour/besan

3 tbsp rice flour

1 tsp ground coriander

2 tsp ground cumin

1 tbsp panch phoron

¼ tsp ground turmeric

¼ tsp chilli powder

handful of fresh coriander/cilantro, very finely chopped

1½ tsp salt

2 tsp sugar

½ tsp black pepper

½ tsp bicarbonate of soda/baking soda

330ml/11¼fl oz/1¼ cups IPA beer, cold

2 large white onions, sliced horizontally into rings

Nisha's Quick Indian Ketchup (page 83), to serve

1 Heat a 5cm/2in depth of oil in a deep-fat fryer or heavy-based saucepan to 180°C/350°F. You'll know it's hot enough when a sprinkling of flour sizzles and floats to the surface.

2 In a large mixing bowl, combine the flours, spices and chopped coriander along with the salt, sugar, black pepper and bicarbonate of soda.

3 Slowly whisk the cold IPA into the dry ingredients until you have a batter the consistency of double cream. Taste for seasoning.

4 Add a handful of onion rings to the batter, turning to coat.

5 When the oil is hot, slowly add the battered onion rings and fry for 3–4 minutes, or until puffed and golden brown. Remove with a slotted spoon to drain on paper towels and repeat with the remaining rings.

6 Serve hot – these need to be eaten immediately or they will soften. I like to serve them with my Indian ketchup!

Beetroot Chops

Chops are a classic Bengali dish – they make perfect snacks or finger food for a party. Nice and spicy, with a pop of colour from the beets and crunch from the peanuts, these are a real conversation starter. Serve with a raita for dipping or a chutney – my Spicy Tomato and Date Chutney on page 85 is ideal. They are best eaten when freshly fried, but can be reheated in the oven at 180°C/350°F/gas mark 4 for 10–15 minutes.

SERVES 4

1 white potato, finely diced
75g/2½oz cooked beetroot/beets
2.5cm/1in piece of fresh ginger, peeled
3 garlic cloves, peeled
2 green chillies
50g/2oz/⅓ cup roasted salted peanuts
1 tsp black pepper
1 tsp ground cumin
½ tsp ground coriander
1 tsp amchur/mango powder
25g/1oz/¼ cup porridge oats
2 tbsp cornflour/cornstarch
small handful of fresh coriander/cilantro, leaves and stalks finely chopped
2 tsp salt, or to taste
40g/1½oz/⅔ cup panko breadcrumbs
vegetable oil, for deep-frying

To serve
lemon wedges, for squeezing
chutney of choice or tomato ketchup

1 Cook the potato in a pan of boiling water for 6–8 minutes, or until tender. Drain well, then return to the pan and mash.

2 Meanwhile, grate the beetroot directly into a large bowl.

3 Blitz the ginger, garlic and chillies in a food processor until finely chopped. Add to the bowl, then use the processor to roughly chop the peanuts and tip these into the bowl too.

4 Add the mashed potatoes, ground spices, amchur, oats, cornflour, chopped coriander and salt and use your hands to mix and bring the mixture together into a ball. Divide the ball into 8 pieces, then shape each into a small log shape – these are your beetroot chops.

5 Cover a large plate with the breadcrumbs, then roll each chop in the breadcrumbs until fully coated. Place in the refrigerator for 15–20 minutes to firm up.

6 Heat a 3–4 cm/1½in depth of oil in a deep pan to 180°C/350°F (or until 1 tsp of panko breadcrumbs added to the oil sizzles and rises quickly to the surface). When hot, carefully add the chops and fry for 4–5 minutes, turning regularly, or until golden brown and crisp. Remove with a slotted spoon to drain on paper towels.

7 Enjoy with lemon wedges for squeezing and your chutney of choice or some ketchup.

Aloo Chops

These delicious little breadcrumbed croquettes come in many forms in India and are very much the street-food vendors' favourite. Always deep-fried and utterly essential to life! Aloo chops dispense with any meat component and are, quite simply, mashed potato balls spiked with green chilli. I love to serve them with Nisha's Green Chutney (page 83) on the side for dipping and a raita works perfectly, too, such as the Beetroot Raita on page 39.

SERVES 4

500g/1lb 2oz potatoes, peeled and cut into small chunks

2 garlic cloves, finely chopped

2.5cm/1in piece of fresh ginger, peeled and finely chopped

1 red onion, finely chopped

1 green chilli, finely chopped

1 tbsp ground cumin

1 tbsp ground coriander

10 fine green beans, finely chopped

2 tsp salt

1 egg

100g/3½oz/generous ¾ cup plain/ all-purpose flour

80g/3oz/1⅓ cups panko breadcrumbs

vegetable oil, for deep-frying

Beetroot Raita (page 39) and Nisha's Green Chutney (page 83), to serve

1 Cook the potatoes in a large pan of boiling salted water for 8–10 minutes, or until very tender. Drain, then return to the pan and mash. Set aside to cool.

2 When it is cool enough to handle, add the garlic, ginger, onion, chilli, ground spices, beans and salt to the mash and mix until thoroughly combined. Taste for seasoning, then divide into 12 balls of equal size and squash lightly to form little puck shapes – these are your "chops".

3 Crack the egg into a shallow bowl and lightly beat. Add the flour to a plate and the panko breadcrumbs to a separate plate. Roll one of the chops in some flour, then dip it into the egg, then into the breadcrumbs and pat until well coated. Place on a plate. Repeat until all the chops are coated, then place in the refrigerator for 15–20 minutes to let them firm up.

4 Meanwhile, heat a 5cm/2in depth of oil in a deep, heavy-based saucepan or deep-fat fryer to 180°C/350°F. You'll know it's hot enough when a sprinkling of breadcrumbs sizzle and quickly float to the surface.

5 Carefully add the chops to the hot oil and fry for 4–5 minutes, turning regularly, until golden brown and crisp (you may need to do this in two batches). Remove with a slotted spoon to a plate lined with paper towels to absorb excess oil.

6 Enjoy hot, with raita and chutney for dipping.

Aloo & Black Gram Chaat

What a flavour explosion! *Aloo chaat* is a gorgeous Indian street food snack made with potatoes, sweet, sour and spicy chutneys and crunchy fried sev. There is a similar version called *chana chaat*, which is made with chickpeas/garbanzo beans. I've combined the two here and switched up the pulses for nutty kala channa (black chickpeas) for a toothsome delight. Nylon sev are deep-fried vermicelli noodles; if you can't find any, Bombay mix works too – at a push.

SERVES 4–6

salt, for the cooking water

600g/1lb 5oz baby potatoes,
    cut into quarters

1 x 400g/14oz can of black chickpeas
    (kala chana), drained and rinsed

4 tbsp Nisha's Green Chutney (page 83)

2 tbsp store-bought tamarind chutney

4 tbsp plain yogurt

2 tsp lemon juice

¼ tsp chilli powder

2 tsp chaat masala

½ tsp salt

½ tsp sugar

a few handfuls of nylon sev (available in Asian
    grocers and some larger supermarkets)

1 small red onion, finely chopped

1 Bring a large pan of salted water to the boil, add the potatoes and cook for 6–8 minutes, or until cooked through with a little bite remaining, then drain and refresh under cold running water until cold.

2 Place the cold, cooked potatoes in a mixing bowl with all the other ingredients, except the sev and red onion, and give it a really good mix. Taste for seasoning, adjusting to your liking.

3 Serve topped with the nylon sev and chopped red onion and enjoy.

South Indian Shallot Curry

Inspired by a South Indian curry called *ulli theeyal*, this is a tangy, spicy dish softened by the sweetness of the shallots and coconut. It is quite a dry, rich curry and is great as a side dish on a table with lots of other dishes, perhaps when entertaining. It works very well alongside something saucier, with some flatbreads for scooping, but can just as well be served with rice, if preferred.

SERVES 2–4

30g/1oz desiccated/dried shredded coconut

vegetable oil, for cooking

400g/14oz banana shallots, peeled
  and halved

1 stalk of fresh curry leaves (about 10–12),
  leaves stripped from stalk

1 tsp black mustard seeds

1 tsp fenugreek seeds

2 tbsp tomato purée/paste

½ tsp red chilli powder

1 tsp ground coriander

1 tsp sugar

3 tsp tamarind paste

150ml/5fl oz/⅔ cup water, or as needed

salt, to taste

flatbreads, to serve

1 Heat a wide non-stick (dry) pan over a medium-low heat. When hot, add the desiccated coconut and cook for 3–4 minutes, stirring regularly, until toasted. Remove to a plate.

2 Reheat the pan over a medium heat and add a drizzle of oil. When hot, place the halved shallots cut-sides down into the pan. Season with salt and cook for 4–5 minutes, or until starting to brown, then flip over and cook for a further 3–4 minutes, or until softening. Remove to the plate with the desiccated coconut.

3 Return the pan to a low heat and add 2 tbsp vegetable oil. When hot, add the curry leaves, mustard seeds and fenugreek seeds and let them sizzle until the fenugreek seeds are just golden brown (do not let them burn), then stir in the tomato purée, chilli powder, ground coriander, sugar and tamarind paste. Add the shallots and toasted coconut back to the pan along with the measured water and cover with a lid. Cook for 6–8 minutes, or until the shallots are soft but still holding their shape, adding a splash more water during cooking if needed.

4 Serve with flatbreads for scooping.

Lazy Potato Curry

Aloo dom was one of my mother's staple curries, made with the crop of new potatoes and tinned tomatoes. I have always felt at odds with the dish. It was the curry she made when she had nothing much in and a general lack of enthusiasm. It was one of the few bones of contention between us! This recipe is a little different to my mother's version. It's a simple dish, but sometimes an uncomplicated, everyday, filling curry is just what's needed, especially when the cupboards are a bit bare. It is easily doubled to serve more.

SERVES 2

1 large red onion, roughly chopped

3 garlic cloves, peeled

2.5cm/1in piece of fresh ginger, peeled

1 green chilli, stems removed

3 tbsp vegetable oil

400g/14oz baby potatoes

1½ tsp salt

1 tsp ground turmeric

1½ tbsp garam masala

1 tsp sugar

2 tbsp tomato purée/paste

150ml/5fl oz/scant ⅔ cup water, or as needed

small bunch of fresh coriander/cilantro, stems and leaves roughly chopped

1 Combine the red onion, garlic, ginger and green chilli in a small food processor and blitz into a paste. Set aside.

2 Heat 2 tbsp of the oil in a large, wide pan that has a lid over a medium heat. Add the baby potatoes with 1 tsp of the salt and ½ tsp of the turmeric. Fry for 5–6 minutes, or until the potato skins start to wrinkle and crisp up, then remove the potatoes to a plate.

3 Return the pan to a medium heat and add the remaining 1 tbsp oil. When hot, add the spice paste and cook for 3–4 minutes, or until fragrant.

4 Add the garam masala with the remaining ½ tsp salt, ½ tsp turmeric and the sugar. Add the tomato purée and measured water, bring to the boil, then add the potatoes back to the pan and turn the heat down to a simmer. Cook, covered, for 8–10 minutes, or until the potatoes are cooked through and tender, stirring regularly and adding more water, if needed.

5 Stir in most of the chopped coriander. Garnish the dish with the remaining coriander just before serving.

Caramelized Onion Dal

Dal is always a dish I associate with comfort food. Nourishing and gentle on the stomach, it's what I turn to when I feel under the weather or just want my meal to give me that warm hug of familiarity. But this dal is something else entirely – the sweet caramelized onions stirred through it bring a feeling of luxury and the crispy onions on top are absolutely the best bit!

SERVES 4

250g/9oz/1 cup red lentils,
200g/7oz/1 cup chopped tomatoes
¼ tsp ground turmeric
1 tsp salt
700ml/24fl oz/3 cups water
1 tbsp vegetable oil
1 tsp nigella seeds
4 garlic cloves, finely sliced
1 green chilli, finely sliced

¼ tsp asafoetida/hing
juice of ½ lemon
small bunch of fresh coriander/cilantro, leaves
    and stems finely chopped

For the caramelized onions

3 tbsp vegetable oil
3 brown onions, finely sliced
1 tsp salt
2 tsp sugar

1 Start by making the caramelized onions. Heat the oil in a wide non-stick frying pan/skillet over a medium heat. When hot, add the onions, salt and sugar, and cook, stirring, for 10–15 minutes, or until the onions are very caramelized but not burned. Turn off the heat and set aside.

2 Meanwhile, combine the lentils, chopped tomatoes, turmeric, salt and measured water in a saucepan and bring to the boil, then reduce to a simmer and cook for 20–25 minutes, or until the lentils are tender.

3 Heat the oil in a separate saucepan over a medium heat. Add the nigella seeds and fry until they start to crackle, then add the garlic and cook for 2–3 minutes. Add the green chilli, asafoetida and two-thirds of the caramelized onions, cook for a further 2–3 minutes, then pour the mixture into the dal pan along with the lemon juice.

4 Serve garnished with the remaining caramelized onions and chopped coriander.

Beetroot Raita

This pretty pink raita is absolutely delicious when served as a dip with Aloo Chops (page 31) or my IPA Onion Rings (page 26). It's also great spread inside the Ruby Wraps (page 173) or Chickpea Kati Roll (page 92) in place of the other yogurt sauces. Earthy, smoky and a real show-stopper on any dinner table.

SERVES 3–4

75g/2½oz cooked beetroot/beets (not packed in vinegar)

1 tbsp vegetable oil

2 tsp ground cumin

1 tsp smoked paprika

1 stalk of fresh curry leaves, leaves stripped

pinch of black pepper

2 tbsp mixed seeds

200g/7oz/generous ¾ cup Greek yogurt

1½ tsp salt, or to taste

juice of ½ lemon

1 Grate the beetroot and place in a sieve/strainer in the sink to drain.

2 Meanwhile, heat the oil in a small non-stick frying pan/skillet over a low heat. When hot, add the cumin, smoked paprika and curry leaves with the black pepper and let sizzle for a minute, then add the mixed seeds and stir for 2–3 minutes, or until toasted.

3 Mix the drained beetroot with the yogurt in your serving bowl and season with salt and lemon juice to taste.

4 Drizzle over the sizzled spices and seed mixture just before serving.

Beetroot & Cauliflower Curry

Packed with flavour and interest, this is an ode to wintery veg. And just look at that colour! Starting off with a classic headnote spicing of cumin seeds with nigella seeds and green chilli, robust and earthy beets can handle the strong finish of the traditional meat spice, garam masala. With a squeeze of lemon juice added at the end for a bit of lift, this is a gorgeous curry for colder days.

SERVES 3–4 AS A SIDE OR
    2 AS A MAIN

3 tbsp vegetable oil

1 heaped tsp panch phoron

1 green chilli, finely sliced

150g/5oz beetroot/beets, peeled and cut
    into 2.5cm/1in cubes

½ cauliflower (about 300g/10½oz),
    broken into small florets, plus a handful of
    cauliflower leaves, roughly chopped

2 tbsp chopped tomatoes

1 tsp ground turmeric

2 tsp ground coriander

¼ tsp chilli powder

1 tsp salt

½ tsp sugar, or to taste

100ml/3½fl oz/scant ½ cup just-boiled water

½ tsp lemon juice

1 tsp garam masala

small bunch of fresh coriander/cilantro, leaves
    and stems roughly chopped

1 Heat the oil in a wide pan that has a lid over a medium heat. When hot, add the panch phoron and cook until the nuggets of fenugreek seeds begin to turn golden, then add the chilli and beetroot and cook, covered, for 6–8 minutes, or until starting to soften.

2 Add the cauliflower florets, chopped cauliflower leaves, chopped tomatoes, ground spices, chilli powder, salt, sugar and hot water, then cover again and cook for a further 10–12 minutes, or until everything is cooked through.

3 Finish with the lemon juice and garam masala, and taste for seasoning.

4 Serve garnished with the chopped coriander.

Manchurian Honey Potatoes

This is a versatile Indo-Chinese recipe that's perfect as a snack, a side dish or "small plate" as part of a larger meal, perhaps if you've got friends round for lunch or dinner and want to serve a few different sharing dishes. It works really well alongside the Lip-Smacking Corn Ribs (page 200), the Aloo and Black Gram Chaat (page 32) and the Samosa Tart (page 116), among others. Crispy potatoes, sticky with honey and spiked with chilli – who could resist? *Pictured opposite top, with Gujarati Turnips and Greens (page 44).*

SERVES 4 AS A SIDE

500g/1lb 2oz baby potatoes, halved

2 tsp cornflour/cornstarch

vegetable oil, for frying

3 garlic cloves, finely sliced

2 spring onions/scallions, finely sliced

pinch of salt

sesame seeds, for sprinkling

For the sauce

2 tbsp tomato purée/paste

2 tbsp honey

2 tbsp soy sauce

1 tsp chilli/hot pepper flakes, or to taste

2 tbsp hot water

1 Bring a saucepan of water to the boil, add the baby potatoes and cook for 5–6 minutes, or until tender to the point of a knife but still holding their shape. Drain in a colander. Place the colander over a bowl, then add the cornflour and gently toss together.

2 Meanwhile, heat a large frying pan/skillet over a medium heat. Add a drizzle of oil, then add the sliced garlic and spring onions and cook for 3–4 minutes, or until softened, then remove with a slotted spoon to a plate.

3 Add another 2 tbsp of oil to the same pan. When hot, add the potatoes with the pinch of salt and cook for 5–6 minutes, turning regularly until crisp all over.

4 Meanwhile, mix together the sauce ingredients in a small bowl.

5 When the potatoes are crispy, add the cooked garlic and spring onions back to the pan along with the sauce, and stir until everything is well coated and sticky.

6 Serve, sprinkled with the sesame seeds.

Gujarati Turnips & Greens

Turnips are a popular ingredient in India and this is a typical way to cook them. You can easily adjust the heat to your own taste, too. It is quite a dry dish, so I find it makes a nice accompaniment to a curry with a bit of a gravy, such as my Squash and Black Chickpea Curry (page 56), the Yellow Dal with Beetroot Leaves (page 106) or the Jackfruit Jalfrezi (page 153). A perfect way to make the most of seasonal winter veg. *Pictured on page 42, bottom.*

SERVES 4

2 tbsp vegetable oil

2 tsp cumin seeds

1 tsp asafoetida/hing

3 garlic cloves, finely sliced

1 red chilli, sliced (deseeded
   if you like it less hot)

1 tbsp tomato purée/paste

300g/10½oz turnips, peeled
   and roughly diced

100ml/3½fl oz/scant ½ cup water,
   or as needed

1½ tsp salt

1 tsp sugar

30g/1oz kale, stalks removed
   and leaves torn

1 Heat the oil in a wide pan that has a lid over a medium heat. When hot, add the cumin seeds and cook until dark brown, then add the asafoetida. Allow to sizzle and become fragrant, then add the garlic and chilli and cook for a couple of minutes, or until starting to soften.

2 Add the tomato purée with the diced turnips and measured water, salt and sugar. Cover with the pan lid and cook for 8–10 minutes, or until softened and cooked with a slight bite.

3 Add the kale and cover again for 3–4 minutes, or until wilted (you might need to add a splash more water at this stage if it looks dry).

4 Taste for seasoning and it's ready to serve.

Spiced Leeks with Channa Dal

This is one of my Aunty Geeta's specialities. I love it because leek is such an overlooked, humble vegetable, yet this is such a simple, delicious recipe. The nutty flavour of roasted channa dal gives the dish a lovely crunch. It is easily halved to serve two.

SERVES 4

3 tbsp vegetable oil

2 tsp nigella seeds

2 large leeks, finely sliced

1 tsp ground turmeric

½ tsp chilli powder

1 tsp salt

1 tsp sugar

juice of ½ lemon

100g/3½oz/scant ½ cup store-bought roasted channa dal (split chickpeas) (or dry-roast your own)

1 Heat the oil in a non-stick frying pan over a medium heat. When hot, add the nigella seeds and fry until they start to crackle, then add the leeks with the spices, salt and sugar. Cook, stirring, for 5–6 minutes, or until softened.

2 Add half of the lemon juice and taste for seasoning, adding in the remaining lemon juice if needed.

3 Serve garnished with the roasted channa dal for a little crunch. Alternatively, you can leave out the channa dal and serve as is.

Carrot & Radish Pickle

This home-style "quick pickle" with carrots and radishes is nice as a tangy side with one of my spicier vegetable curries – or even served alongside a dal and rice. It's light, crunchy and fresh when eaten immediately, but if you keep it in the refrigerator for a few days, the flavours mellow and the veg soften to create a delectable relish that is great in sandwiches or even used to top burgers.

MAKES 1 LARGE JAR

3 carrots, peeled and cut into thin batons

100g/3½oz radishes, halved

300ml/10½fl oz/1¼ cups vegetable oil

1 tsp fenugreek seeds, crushed in a pestle and mortar or spice grinder

3 tsp mustard seeds

½ tsp asafoetida/hing

1 tsp ground turmeric

½ tsp sugar

3 tsp salt

juice of ½ lemon

1 Add the carrot batons and radish halves to a bowl, cover with boiling water and leave for 10 minutes.

2 Meanwhile, heat the oil in a small saucepan over a medium-low heat. When hot, remove from the heat, then add the fenugreek and mustard seeds, asafoetida and turmeric. Set aside to cool.

3 Drain the carrots and radishes, then add them to a sterilized jar along with the sugar and salt, stirring well.

4 When the spiced oil has cooled, pour this over the top of the carrots and radishes and add the lemon juice. Stir again and taste for seasoning.

5 You can eat it straight away, but it is better to leave it for a few days to let the flavours infuse. Stored in the refrigerator, it should keep for 10–12 days.

2
GOURDS

I have a passionate devotion to this group of veg, of which there is such wondrous variety in summer and autumn. Grown on rubbish heaps in India, they are widely available – the ultimate humble veg, yet so royally sweet and generous. The luxurious flesh of pumpkins and squashes quickly takes on spicy flavours, as do courgettes/zucchini, which grow so abundantly. Cucumbers, also in this group, bring essential freshness and lightness to Indian meals, in salads or raitas.

Cucumber, Ginger & Lime Salad

Simple, refreshing, cleansing, I can't get enough of this cooling green salad. Although the kick of ginger gives it a bit of tongue-tingling interest, it's ideal served on the side of any spicy dish for dousing the fires.

SERVES 4 AS A SIDE

1 cucumber

handful of fresh coriander/cilantro, stems and leaves finely chopped

handful of fresh mint, leaves finely chopped and stems discarded

1cm/½in piece of fresh ginger, peeled and finely grated

1 tsp olive oil

juice of 1 lime

½ tsp black salt (kala namak)

1 Roughly chop the cucumber into small bite-size pieces and place in a mixing bowl with the chopped herbs and grated ginger.

2 Stir in the olive oil and lime juice, then add the black salt.

3 Taste for seasoning before serving.

Tangy Tamarind Roasted Squash

Sweet and sour flavours work so beautifully with the luxurious flesh of the butternut squash. This is a dry dish, so I find it works well when served with more saucy dishes, such as my Yellow Dal with Beetroot Leaves (page 106), any of the egg curries or the Jackfruit Jalfrezi (page 153). It is also beautiful on its own, as a simple lunch dish, with a creamy raita and some salad alongside.

SERVES 4 AS A SIDE

1 small butternut squash (about 800g/
    1lb 12oz), peeled and cut into
    large chunks
4 tbsp vegetable oil
1 tbsp panch phoran
1 tsp asafoetida/hing
1 tsp chilli flakes

1 tsp ground turmeric
2 tbsp tamarind paste
2 tbsp jaggery or brown sugar
2 tsp ground coriander
1 tsp amchur/mango powder
1 tsp salt
juice of ½ lemon
handful of fresh coriander/cilantro, to garnish

1 In a large bowl, combine the squash with all the other ingredients, except the lemon juice and coriander, and stir to combine. Leave to marinate for 15–30 minutes, or longer if you have the time.

2 Meanwhile, preheat the oven to 180°C/350°F/gas mark 4.

3 Arrange the marinated squash over a large baking sheet or roasting pan, then roast for 25–30 minutes, or until cooked through, stirring every 10 minutes to ensure even roasting.

4 Serve garnished with lemon juice and coriander.

Indian Courgette Fries

Running out of ideas for what to do with ALL those courgettes/zucchini that come with the season's glut? If you've already tried my Courgette Kofta Curry (page 58) and made a few batches of my Quick Pickled Courgettes (page 63), then why not give these little treats a whirl instead of your usual potato fries. Coated in a light and crunchy spiced batter, they taste out of this world with a spicy mayo (try my Green Chilli Mayo on page 200) or dipped into a raita or chutney.

SERVES 4–6

vegetable oil, for deep-frying

50g/2oz/scant ½ cup plain/
    all-purpose flour

50g/2oz/½ cup gram flour/besan

30g/1oz/3 tbsp rice flour

½ tsp bicarbonate of soda/baking soda

1 tsp salt

1 tsp cumin seeds

¼ tsp chilli powder

1 tsp ground turmeric

1 tsp ground cumin

100–150ml/3½–5fl oz/scant ½–⅔ cup cold
    sparkling water

2 large courgettes/zucchini, cut into
    thin batons

mayo, or your favourite chutney or raita,
    to serve

1 Heat a 5cm/2in depth of oil in a deep, heavy-based saucepan or deep-fat fryer to 180°C/350°F. You'll know it's hot enough when you can add a piece of bread or a sprinkling of flour and it sizzles and floats to the surface.

2 Combine all the dried ingredients in a large bowl, then slowly pour in the sparkling water, whisking lightly to bring it together until the batter is the consistency of double/heavy cream. You may not need all of the water. Taste for seasoning.

3 Add the courgette batons to the batter and turn until all are coated.

4 Working in batches, carefully add a handful of the courgette batons to the hot oil. Try to separate them between your fingers as you add them so they don't all clump together. Fry until golden brown and crisp, then remove with a slotted spoon to drain on paper towels. Repeat until all are cooked.

5 Serve hot, with some mayo or your favourite chutney or raita.

Squash & Black Chickpea Curry

This squash curry is a typical Bengali dish, although pumpkin would be more generally used in India, and is thick, sweet and very filling. Black chickpeas, or kala channa, are quite common in Indian cooking and they make a nice change from regular chickpeas/ garbanzo beans, giving the dish a slightly nutty flavour. They are slightly higher in fibre and iron, too, so make a very nutritious addition. Serve with flatbreads (try my Bengali Plain Flour Puris on page 209).

SERVES 4

2 tbsp vegetable oil

1 dried red chilli

1 tbsp panch phoron

1 tsp asafoetida/hing

5cm/2in piece of fresh ginger, peeled and finely chopped

1 small butternut squash, peeled and chopped into large bite-size chunks

2 tsp ground cumin

2 tsp ground coriander

¼ tsp chilli powder

½ tsp ground turmeric

400ml/14fl oz/1⅔ cups boiling water

1 tsp sugar

2 tsp salt

400g/14oz canned black chickpeas/ kala channa, drained and rinsed

1 tsp garam masala

1 Heat the oil in a wide saucepan that has a lid over a medium heat. When hot, add the dried red chilli and panch phoron and let sizzle until golden brown. Take care not to burn them.

2 Stir in the asafoetida and chopped ginger, then add the butternut squash. Stir to combine.

3 Add all of the ground spices (except the garam masala), then pour in the freshly boiled water. Add the sugar and salt, cover with the pan lid and simmer for 15 minutes, or until the squash is almost cooked through.

4 Add the black chickpeas along with the garam masala, cover again and cook for a further 10 minutes, or until the squash and chickpeas are both cooked through.

Courgette Kofta Curry

These golden veggie koftas cloaked in coconutty masala are just gorgeous. You definitely need a flatbread to soak up all the beautiful sauce. A rich and inviting summertime curry.

SERVES 4

For the kofta
800g/1lb 12oz courgettes/zucchini
1½ tsp salt
50g/2oz/scant ½ cup cornflour/cornstarch
150g/5oz/1½ cups gram flour/besan
2 tsp ajwain/lovage seeds
½ tsp ground turmeric
vegetable oil, for deep-frying

For the curry
3 tbsp vegetable oil
2 brown onions, finely chopped
3 garlic cloves, finely chopped

5cm/2in piece of fresh ginger, peeled and
   finely chopped
1 green chilli, finely chopped
5 curry leaves
1 tsp ground turmeric
¼ tsp chilli powder
2 tbsp garam masala
2 tsp ground coriander
2 tsp ground cumin
2 tsp salt
1 tsp sugar
1 x 400ml/14fl oz can of coconut milk
150ml/5fl oz/⅔ cup boiling water
juice of ½ lemon

1 Grate the courgettes and place in a sieve/strainer set over a bowl. Sprinkle with 1 tsp of the salt and set aside to drain for at least 30 minutes, ideally 1–2 hours.

2 Meanwhile, start the curry. Heat the oil in a medium saucepan over a medium heat. When hot, add the onions and cook for 7–8 minutes, or until golden brown. Add the garlic, ginger and chilli, and cook for 2 minutes. Then add the spices, salt and sugar. Stir in the coconut milk and boiling water and bring to a simmer. Cook for 6–8 minutes, or until slightly thickened.

3 Squeeze the remaining water from the courgettes, then transfer the pulp to a mixing bowl. Add the cornflour, gram flour, ajwain, turmeric and remaining ½ tsp of salt, and mix well.

4 Heat a 5cm/2in depth of oil in a deep-fat fryer or heavy-based saucepan to 180°C/ 350°F, or until a small piece of bread added to the oil sizzles and floats to the surface.

5 Use a teaspoon to drop small balls of the courgette batter into the hot oil (you may need to work in batches). Cook for 2–3 minutes, or until golden brown. Remove with a slotted spoon to a plate lined with paper towels to absorb excess oil.

6 Add the fried kofta to the sauce along with the lemon juice (and possibly a little more water to get the consistency you want). Adjust the seasoning to taste and serve.

Pumpkin, Ginger & Spinach Curry

Fenugreek seeds, especially when paired with asafoetida/hing, pack some serious clout and really wake up quiet, watery vegetables, such as squashes or pumpkin. This glorious orange curry is given an iron-rich hit of spinach and some punchy ginger too, so it's wonderfully good for you as well as tasty.

SERVES 2–4

4 tbsp vegetable oil

½ tsp fenugreek seeds

¼ tsp asafoetida/hing

1 small pumpkin, peeled, deseeded and cut into chunks (around 800g/1lb 12oz peeled weight)

1 tsp ground turmeric

¼ tsp chilli powder

1 tsp salt

1 tsp sugar

100ml/3½fl oz/scant ½ cup water, or more as needed

150g/5oz baby spinach

5cm/2in piece of fresh ginger, peeled and grated

2 tsp garam masala

juice of ½ lemon

1 Heat the oil in a large wide-based pan that has a lid over a medium heat. When hot, add the fenugreek seeds and cook until the nuggets of fenugreek turn dark brown. Be careful not to burn, as they will taste bitter. Add the asafoetida to the pan, followed by the chopped pumpkin, turmeric, chilli powder, salt and sugar and stir until well combined. Then add the measured water and bring almost to the boil, before reducing to a simmer and covering. Let simmer for 20–25 minutes, or until the pumpkin is almost cooked through.

2 Add the spinach, grated ginger and garam masala and cook for a final 5 minutes until the spinach is wilted and the pumpkin is cooked through.

3 Finish with the lemon juice and taste for seasoning before serving, adding a splash more water if it is a little too dry for your liking.

Butternut Squash Dry-Fry

The simplest of preparations, this squash dry-fry makes a perfect side dish to any of my curries, or can form part of a selection of small sharing dishes for an Indian feast.

SERVES 2

5 tbsp vegetable oil

2 tsp mustard seeds

1 small butternut squash (600g/1lb 5oz peeled weight), deseeded and cut into 2.5cm/1in chunks

1 tsp salt

¼ tsp red chilli powder

1 tsp ground turmeric

juice of ½ lemon

1 Heat the oil in a wide-based pan that has a lid over a medium heat. When hot, add the mustard seeds and let them sizzle until fragrant, then add the chopped squash. Stir to coat in the oil, before adding the salt, chilli powder and turmeric. Cover and cook for 10–12 minutes, or until the squash is cooked through.

2 Add the lemon juice and taste for seasoning before serving.

Quick Pickled Courgettes

I love quick pickles, served when the veg still has a bit of bite and freshness. However, the advantage of leaving these pickles to marinate for a few days is that the flavours mellow and seep into the vegetables. Either way, they are delicious. Pickles make the perfect side to many Indian dishes, which is why you will find them served at nearly every meal, almost like a condiment, bringing a piquant edge to tantalize our taste buds.

MAKES A 1L/35FL OZ JAR

100ml/3½fl oz/scant ½ cup vegetable oil

1 tsp nigella seeds

½ tsp fenugreek seeds

3 garlic cloves, sliced

1 long red chilli, chopped

¼ tsp ground turmeric

½ tsp asafoetida/hing

2 large courgettes/zucchini, cut into
   small batons

2 tsp salt

1 tsp sugar

juice of 3 lemons

1 Heat the oil in a wide, non-stick frying pan over a medium heat. When hot, add the nigella and fenugreek seeds and let them sizzle briefly. Add the garlic, chilli, turmeric and asafoetida, and cook for 2 minutes, stirring, then remove from the heat.

2 Place the courgette batons in a heatproof bowl and pour over the spiced oil. Add the salt, sugar and lemon juice and stir until well combined.

3 Taste for seasoning and let cool.

4 This can be eaten immediately, but will benefit from a day or two to marinate. Store in a sterilized jar in the fridge for up to one week.

Pumpkin Halwa

You might have tried a carrot halwa pudding before, but what about pumpkin? This has the autumnal flavours of pumpkin spice latte and is completely vegan. It can easily be made ahead of time. However, it will thicken as it cools, so when reheating, add some water to loosen. Sweet and aromatic, it's like a comforting hug in dessert form.

SERVES 4

500g/1lb 2oz pumpkin (peeled and deseeded weight)
400ml/14fl oz canned coconut milk
1 tsp mixed spice
½ tsp ground ginger
80–100g/3–3½oz/⅓–scant ½ cup brown sugar
handful of pistachios, roughly chopped

1 Grate the pumpkin coarsely using a box grater.

2 Heat a large heavy-based saucepan over a medium heat. When hot, add the grated pumpkin, coconut milk, mixed spice and ground ginger. Fill the empty coconut can with water and add this in too. Add 80g/3oz/⅓ cup of the brown sugar and give everything a good mix. Cook for 30–40 minutes, or until thickened to a porridge consistency.

3 Taste for seasoning, adding the remaining 20g/¾oz/2 tbsp brown sugar if needed.

4 Serve warm, decorated with the chopped pistachios.

3

NIGHTSHADES

The evocative name of this summer-cropping vegetable family belies their nature – these are veg that ripen to perfection in the hot sun. And every one of the nightshade family is an essential ingredient in the Indian kitchen. Aubergines/eggplant, capsicums/bell peppers, tomatoes and chillies – where would our cuisine be without them? Aubergines, in particular, hold a talismanic value for us.

Aunty Geeta's Cur-heee with Crispy Okra

This family recipe is one of my Aunty Geeta's all-time favourites. *Cur-heee* (or *kadhi*) is a Gujarati thick and fragrant yogurt soup, here topped with crunchy fried discs of cumin-spiked okra. I serve it with a roti-style flatbread to scoop it straight into my mouth – delicious!

SERVES 4

200g/7oz/generous ¾ cup plain yogurt

¼ tsp ground turmeric

4 tbsp gram flour/besan

2 garlic cloves, finely chopped

12 fresh curry leaves

¼ tsp chilli powder

1 tsp salt

1 tsp sugar

small bunch of fresh coriander/cilantro, finely chopped

300ml/10½ fl oz/1¼ cups water

For the crispy okra topping

1 tbsp vegetable oil

1 tsp mustard seeds

175g/6oz okra, finely sliced

½ tsp salt

2 tsp ground cumin

1 In a large, heavy saucepan, combine the yogurt, turmeric, gram flour, garlic, curry leaves, chilli powder, salt, sugar and chopped coriander, then slowly whisk in the water. Taste for seasoning, then set the pan over a medium heat. Cook for 6–8 minutes, stirring very regularly, or until thickened.

2 Meanwhile, make the crispy okra topping. Heat the oil in a small non-stick frying pan/skillet over a medium heat. When hot, add the mustard seeds and let sizzle briefly. Then add the sliced okra, salt and ground cumin and cook for 6–8 minutes, or until softened and browned.

3 Divide the *cur-heee* between 4 bowls and pour over the okra mixture just before serving. Enjoy.

Fried Aubergine With Mustard Yogurt

Aubergine/eggplant is certainly India's best-loved vegetable, possibly because it behaves similarly to meat, both in texture and its ability to soak up spices – useful in a heavily vegan population. Inspired by a Bengali dish called *begun bhaja*, these crispy fried aubergines work really well as a snack or starter. Remember not to overcrowd the aubergines in the pan or they won't crisp up nicely. The mustard yogurt can be made ahead of time, but the aubergines need to be fried just before serving or they'll start to go soggy. They are also nice served on a roti and rolled like a wrap.

SERVES 4

1 large aubergine/eggplant, sliced into
    5mm/¼in rounds
1 tsp ground turmeric
½ tsp chilli powder
50g/2oz/¼ cup rice flour
20g/¾oz/⅛ cup gram flour/besan
vegetable oil, for deep-frying
small handful of fresh coriander/cilantro,
    leaves and stalks roughly chopped
salt, to taste

For the mustard yogurt

drizzle of vegetable oil
2.5cm/1in piece of fresh ginger, peeled and
    finely chopped
1–2 green chillies, finely chopped
1 tsp English mustard paste
¼ tsp ground turmeric
½ tsp salt
pinch of sugar
150g/5oz/scant ⅔ cup plain yogurt
juice of ½ lime

1 Place the aubergine slices in a bowl, add the ground turmeric and chilli powder and season generously with salt. Toss to combine and set aside to marinate for 10 minutes.

2 Meanwhile, make the mustard yogurt. Heat a drizzle of oil in a small frying pan/skillet over a medium heat. When hot, add the chopped ginger and green chillies. Cook for 2–3 minutes, or until softened, then transfer to a small bowl. Stir in the mustard paste, ground turmeric, salt, sugar, yogurt and lime juice. Set aside.

3 Combine the rice flour and gram flour on a large plate and set aside.

4 Heat a 3–4cm/1½in depth of oil in a deep pan to 180°C/350°F.

5 Coat the aubergine slices in the flour mixture. When the oil is hot, add the slices in batches and cook for 4–5 minutes, or until crispy. Remove with a slotted spoon to drain on paper towels.

6 Serve the crispy aubergine slices on a plate, sprinkled with the coriander, and put the mustard yogurt on the side.

Punjabi Padron Peppers

This is my Indian twist on a classic Spanish tapas. It's nice to have with drinks or as an *amuse bouche* to the rest of your meal. Alternatively, if you're serving a sharing feast with lots of snacky bits, this can feature nicely.

SERVES 4

1 tbsp vegetable oil or sunflower oil

130g/4½oz Padron peppers

1 tsp chaat masala

½ tsp salt

1 Heat a large non-stick frying pan/skillet over a medium–high heat and add the oil. When hot, add the Padron peppers in an even layer. When they start sizzling, stir and cook for a further 3–4 minutes, or until they are slightly charred all over.

2 Remove the charred peppers to a serving dish and sprinkle with the chaat masala and salt. Serve immediately.

Bengali Aubergine Bharta

This is basically a spiced aubergine/eggplant purée – if you like *baba ghanoush*, you'll love this. It's a very traditional and popular dish in India, and is amazing served with rice or flatbreads. Flame your aubergines first to get the flesh all smoky, then mash it into a sauce of fresh tomatoes, ginger, mustard oil and green chillies, to make a punchy dip (or side dish) that will blow your mind.

SERVES 2

2 aubergines/eggplant
2 tbsp mustard oil or vegetable oil
1 brown onion, finely chopped
2.5cm/1in piece of fresh ginger, peeled
   and finely chopped
3 garlic cloves, finely chopped

1 green chilli, finely chopped
1 tsp salt
1 tsp ground coriander
¼ tsp ground turmeric
2 tomatoes, finely chopped
handful of fresh coriander/cilantro,
   leaves and stems finely chopped

1 Preheat the grill/broiler to high and line the grill pan or a baking sheet with foil.

2 Prick the aubergines all over with a fork and place on the foil-lined tray. Grill/broil, turning regularly, for 10–15 minutes, or until blackened all over. Remove from the grill and set aside to cool slightly.

3 When the aubergines are cool enough to handle, remove the skins and scoop out the flesh into a bowl, mashing with a fork.

4 Heat a medium saucepan over a medium heat and add the mustard oil. When hot, add the onion and cook for 4–5 minutes, or until softened.

5 Add the ginger, garlic and green chilli, and cook for 2 minutes, or until fragrant, then add the salt, spices and chopped tomatoes and stir to combine. Cook for a further 2–3 minutes, or until starting to soften.

6 Add the mashed aubergine, stir until hot, then garnish with the chopped coriander and serve.

Okra & Potato Dry-Fry

Okra are such an essential ingredient in India that I am always amazed at how little they are revered in the West. I realize that this is largely to do with their slimy reputation, but when they are cooked properly this is not something to be afraid of. This delicious dry-fry makes a wonderful side dish to a sharing feast and it is the dryness of the fry that is the key to its success – keep cooking the okra until all that sliminess has disappeared and you are left with something sensational.

SERVES 2

200g/7oz baby potatoes, chopped into
    bite-size pieces
6 tbsp vegetable oil
2 tsp cumin seeds
2 tsp mustard seeds
2.5cm/1in piece of fresh ginger, peeled
    and finely chopped
2 garlic cloves, finely chopped
1 tsp ground coriander
¼ tsp ground turmeric
¼ tsp chilli powder
½ tsp salt
1 tsp sugar
1 medium tomato, finely chopped
3 tbsp water
100g/3½oz okra, topped and tailed
½ tsp amchur/mango powder
1 tsp garam masala
juice of ½ lemon

1 Place the potatoes in a pan, cover with water and bring to the boil, then reduce to a simmer and cook for 5–6 minutes, or until tender but still holding their shape. Drain and set aside.

2 Heat 3 tbsp of the oil in a wide pan that has a lid over a medium heat. When hot, add the cumin and mustard seeds and cook until dark brown, then add the ginger and garlic, and cook for 2–3 minutes, or until starting to soften. Add the ground spices, salt, sugar, chopped tomato and water and cook for another minute. Remove from the heat.

3 Heat the remaining 3 tbsp of oil in a separate pan over a medium–high heat. When hot, add the okra and fry until golden brown and all the sliminess has gone, for about 8 minutes.

4 Add the okra and potatoes to the spice pan along with the amchur, garam masala and lemon juice, and cook for a final 5 minutes, or until everything is cooked through.

5-Spice Okra

I am such a huge fan of okra that I had to give you another recipe to showcase how great they can be. Simply cooked in a sauce with a panch phoron spice base, this curry can be enjoyed on its own or as a tasty side dish.

SERVES 2

5 tbsp vegetable oil

2 tsp panch phoron

2 garlic cloves, finely sliced

2 green chillies, finely sliced

2 tsp ground cumin

2 tsp ground coriander

1 tsp ground turmeric

1 tsp salt

1 tsp sugar

2 tbsp tomato purée/paste

100ml/3½fl oz/scant ½ cup water

100g/3½oz okra, halved lengthways

juice of ½ lemon

1 Heat 2 tbsp of the oil in a deep non-stick frying pan/skillet that has a lid over a medium heat. When hot, add the panch phoron and cook until the nuggets of fenugreek turn dark brown. Be careful not to burn, as it will taste bitter.

2 Add the garlic and green chillies, and cook for 1–2 minutes, or until starting to soften, then add the ground spices, salt, sugar and tomato purée.

3 Pour in the water, stirring as you go, until a sauce forms.

4 Meanwhile, heat the remaining 3 tbsp of oil in a separate pan set over a medium–high heat. When hot, add the okra and fry until golden brown and all the sliminess has gone.

5 Add the cooked okra to the sauce and simmer for a final 7–8 minutes, then add the lemon juice, taste for seasoning and serve.

Aubergine Dhansak

This is a vegetarian take on the classic Parsi dish of meat (usually mutton) cooked in a lentil and vegetable base, known as *dhansak*. The Parsi community originally migrated from Persia to India, settling on the coast of Gujarat. Their cuisine still heavily reflects their ancient Persian origins. Hearty and comforting, a good *dhansak* should be spicy, tangy and a little sweet. Here, aubergine/eggplant replaces the traditional mutton and soaks up the flavours of the sauce just as beautifully. It can easily be eaten on its own or with some chapatis and brown rice. A simple *kachumber* (onion and cucumber salad) makes a perfect side dish.

SERVES 4

100g/3½oz/scant ½ cup dried red lentils

3 garlic cloves

2.5cm/1in piece of fresh ginger

3 tbsp vegetable oil

1 cinnamon stick

1 red onion, finely chopped

1 large aubergine/eggplant, finely chopped

1 potato, finely chopped

1 tsp salt, or as needed

2 tomatoes, roughly chopped

1 tbsp tomato purée/paste

1 tsp ground cumin

1 tsp ground coriander

¼ tsp chilli powder

½ tsp ground turmeric

1 tsp sugar, or as needed

up to 450ml/15fl oz/scant 2 cups boiling water

2 handfuls of kale, leaves only, torn

juice of ½ lemon

2 tsp garam masala

1 In a bowl, cover the dried lentils with boiling water and leave to soak for 20 minutes.

2 Blitz the garlic and ginger to a fine paste in a food processor.

3 Meanwhile, heat the oil in a large, wide pan that has a lid over a medium heat. When hot, add the cinnamon and stir for 30 seconds, or until fragrant, then add the red onion. Cook for 4–5 minutes, then stir in the garlic and ginger paste and cook for a further minute. Add the chopped aubergine and potato with the salt and stir together before adding the chopped tomatoes, tomato purée, spices and the sugar. Cover with the pan lid and cook for 8–10 minutes, or until the vegetables start to soften.

4 Add the lentils, plus their soaking liquid, and 350ml/12fl oz/scant 1½ cups of the boiling water to the pan. Cover and simmer for a further 10–15 minutes, or until the lentils and vegetables are cooked and soft. Keep an eye on the water level and don't let it get too dry.

5 Stir in the kale until wilted, then add the lemon juice and garam masala. Before serving, taste for seasoning, adding salt or sugar, as needed. Add more water if it's looking a bit dry.

Aubergine & White Poppy Seed Curry

This is a twist on my long-cherished recipe for Aubergine with Nigella and Poppy Seed (the original recipe for which can be found in my previous book, *The Spice Tree*). Here, I have removed the tomato element and tweaked the spicing a little for a dry curry that really lets the flavour of the aubergine/eggplant shine through. Ground white poppy seeds are a Bengali kitchen secret. Often combined with mustard, their nutty flavour transforms vegetable dishes into something truly special.

SERVES 2

3 tbsp vegetable oil

1 tsp nigella seeds

1 green chilli, finely chopped

1 aubergine/eggplant, chopped into
 bite-size chunks

2 tsp white poppy seeds

2 tsp just-boiled water

1 tsp ground turmeric

½ tsp chilli powder

1 tsp salt

½ tsp mustard paste

1 tsp sugar

juice of ½ lemon

4–6 tbsp cold water

1 Heat the oil in a wide pan that has a lid over a medium heat. When hot, add the nigella seeds. Fry until they start to crackle and become fragrant, then add the chilli (be careful of spluttering oil – cover with a lid, if needed). Then add the aubergine chunks and fry for 3–4 minutes, or until browned all over.

2 Meanwhile, grind the poppy seeds with the hot water in a pestle and mortar (or in a powerful food processor or spice grinder) until you have a rough paste.

3 When the aubergines have coloured, add the poppy seed paste to the pan along with the turmeric, chilli powder and salt. Add the mustard paste, sugar and lemon juice along with 4 tbsp of the cold water, then cover and cook for a further 6–8 minutes, or until the aubergines are cooked through, adding more water as needed if the pan gets too dry.

Tomato & Nigella Seed Salad

A tomato and onion salad is an essential on every Indian dining table. Sometimes, it can be as simple as the veg just chopped up and tossed together, but to take it to another level I like to spice things up with some earthy nigella seeds and some citrussy chaat masala. This is a cheat's way to quickly pickle the shallots, softening them and taking away some of that raw acidic edge. Ideally, make this in season when tomatoes are at their sweet and juicy best.

SERVES 4 AS A SIDE

1 banana shallot, peeled and finely sliced

juice of ½ lemon

½ tsp sugar

250g/9oz cherry tomatoes, halved

2 tsp olive oil

2 tsp nigella seeds

1 tsp chaat masala

salt, to taste

1 Boil the kettle.

2 Place the sliced shallots into a sieve/strainer, then pour over the boiling water. Let drain fully, then rinse under cold running water.

3 Transfer the shallots to a small mixing bowl and add the lemon juice, a pinch of salt and the sugar. Set aside for 10 minutes.

4 Add the cherry tomatoes to the shallots, then add the olive oil. Taste for seasoning.

5 Serve, garnished with the nigella seeds and chaat masala.

Nisha's Green Chutney

This zingy combination of fresh coriander/cilantro and mint, spiked with the heat of green chillies, will bring an Indian feast together in the most amazing way.

SERVES 4

small bunch of fresh coriander/cilantro

small bunch of fresh mint, leaves only

1 green chilli

¼ brown onion, roughly chopped

1cm/½in piece of fresh ginger, peeled

1½ tsp ground cumin

1 tsp ground coriander

juice of ½ lemon

1 tsp tamarind concentrate

2–3 tsp sugar

1½ tsp salt

1 Add all the ingredients, except the sugar and salt, to a high-speed blender and blitz until smooth. Add the sugar and salt gradually, blitzing and tasting as you go, until the chutney is seasoned to your liking.

Nisha's Quick Indian Ketchup

SERVES 4

150g/5oz store-bought tomato ketchup

small bunch of fresh coriander/cilantro, leaves and stems roughly chopped

2 garlic cloves, finely chopped

½ tsp ground cumin

½ tsp freshly ground black pepper

¼ tsp chilli powder

1 tsp chaat masala

1 tbsp water

1 Blitz everything together in a high-speed blender until smooth. Taste for seasoning.

Spicy Tomato & Date Chutney

This tasty, fruity chutney can be eaten with so many things: eggs, cheese on toast, with curry or rice, with my Beetroot Chops (on page 28) … the list goes on and on.

MAKES A 200ML/7FL OZ JAR

1 tbsp vegetable oil

2 tsp black mustard seeds

2 tsp sesame seeds

2.5cm/1in cinnamon stick

1 tsp chilli powder

5cm/2in piece of fresh ginger, peeled
   and finely chopped (or grated)

5 tomatoes, finely chopped

1 tsp salt

10 pitted dates, finely chopped

2 tbsp tamarind paste

100g/3½oz/½ cup brown sugar

1 Heat the oil in a medium non-stick saucepan over a medium heat. When hot, add the mustard seeds, sesame seeds and cinnamon and let sizzle.

2 Once sizzling, add the chilli powder and chopped ginger, and cook for 2–3 minutes, or until fragrant. Add the chopped tomatoes and salt, and cook for about 5 minutes to let the tomatoes break down, then add the chopped dates, tamarind paste and brown sugar.

3 Keep cooking for 10–15 minutes, stirring regularly until thickened into a jammy chutney consistency.

4 Remove from the heat and let cool, then pour into a sterilized jar and store in the refrigerator for 2–3 weeks.

Maa's Green Chilli Pickle

Quite simply a classic, this is my Maa's searingly hot recipe for chilli pickle. A little different to the chilli pickle you may have seen in my other Mowgli books, this is still very spicy – you have been warned!

MAKES 1 SMALL JAR

100ml/3 ½fl oz/scant ½ cup vegetable oil

1 tbsp panch phoron

25 green chillies, finely chopped or blitzed
    in a food processor

1 tsp ground turmeric

1 tsp salt

juice of 1 lemon

1 Heat 3 tbsp of the oil in a saucepan over a medium–low heat. When hot, add half of the panch phoron and let it sizzle briefly. Be careful not to let it burn or it will taste bitter. Remove from the heat and add the chopped green chillies, turmeric and salt. Beware of spluttering!

2 Return the pan to a low heat and let the mixture cook down for 20–30 minutes, or until the chillies have really softened.

3 Meanwhile, in a separate dry frying pan/skillet, toast the remaining panch phoron for 3–4 minutes, or until fragrant. Let cool, then blitz to a fine powder in a spice grinder or small food processor.

4 Once the chillies have really softened, remove from the heat, stir in the ground panch phoron and transfer to a sterilized jar.

5 Heat the remaining oil until hot, then pour it over the chillies in the jar until they are submerged. Stir in the lemon juice, seal and leave to cool. Store in the refrigerator for up to 6 weeks.

4
BEANS, PEAS & LENTILS

Robust legumes are a must in the meat-free kitchen. These powerhouses of protein do a lot of heavy lifting to produce nourishing, thrifty and delicious meals. Lighter split pulses are quick to cook, easy to digest and make wonderful dals, whereas heavier pulses, such as chickpeas and beans, are so versatile they work in dishes from snacks to accompaniments to curries or breads.

Sweet & Sour Chickpea Chaat

Another street food classic, chickpea/garbanzo bean *chaat* can be found all over India and is quite essential for all-day snacking. It also makes a really fun starter to an Indian feast. Mowgli fans will be familiar with my Yogurt Chat Bombs – this is basically the deconstructed version. You can mix up the toppings to suit your own taste, building your own *chaat* bowl at the table. This is something I'm always a huge fan of – make it yours!

SERVES 2

2 tbsp vegetable oil

1 tsp cumin seeds

1 red onion, finely chopped

1 small potato (about 100g/3½oz), finely chopped

2 tsp ground coriander

2 tsp ground cumin

1 tsp ground turmeric

¼ tsp chilli powder

1 tsp salt

1 x 400g/14oz can chickpeas/garbanzo beans, drained and rinsed

150ml/5fl oz/⅔ cup water

small bunch of fresh coriander/cilantro, stems and leaves finely chopped

juice of 1 lemon

1 tsp sugar

1 tsp garam masala

Toppings:

2 green chillies, finely sliced

1 tomato, finely chopped

4–5 tbsp nylon sev

2 tsp black salt (kala namak) (optional)

2 tbsp tamarind sauce (optional)

1 Heat the oil in a medium saucepan that has a lid over a medium heat. When hot, add the cumin seeds and cook until dark brown, then add half of the red onion. Cook for 5 minutes, or until softened, then add the chopped potato with the ground spices and salt.

2 Add the chickpeas and measured water and cook, covered, for 15 minutes, or until the vegetables are cooked through.

3 Stir through the chopped coriander, lemon juice, sugar and garam masala.

4 To serve, spoon into bowls and let everyone help themselves to the toppings. Enjoy on its own or with Bengali Plain Flour Puris (see page 209).

Chickpea Kati Rolls

Kati rolls were born in Kolkata and have become a popular street food that has started to spread further afield. On a basic level, they are filled flatbreads and fillings come in many shapes and forms, but I like this simple spiced chickpea/garbanzo bean topping wrapped up with some herbs, salad and plenty of piquant sauces. They are also delicious with a fried egg thrown into the mix! The Indian Green Chopped Salad (page 122) goes beautifully with this recipe.

MAKES 4

3 tbsp vegetable oil

1 tsp cumin seeds

1 red onion, finely chopped

3 garlic cloves, finely chopped

1 tsp ground turmeric

1 tsp ground cumin

1 tsp ground coriander

1 tbsp tomato purée/paste

4 tbsp chopped tomatoes

1 tsp salt

½ tsp sugar

1 x 400g/14oz can of chickpeas/garbanzo
    beans, drained and rinsed

2 tsp garam masala

½ tsp chaat masala

juice of ½ lemon

large handful of fresh coriander/cilantro,
    leaves and stalks roughly chopped

4 rotis or parathas

To serve

tamarind chutney

Nisha's Green Chutney (page 83) or Indian
    Green Chopped Salad (page 122)

plain yogurt

1 Heat the oil in a small pan that has a lid over a medium heat. When hot, add the cumin seeds and cook until dark brown, then add the onion and garlic and cook for 4–5 minutes, or until softened.

2 Stir in the ground spices, tomato purée and chopped tomatoes, then add the salt, sugar and drained chickpeas with a splash of water. Cover and cook for 4–5 minutes, or until the chickpeas are softened.

3 Add the garam masala, chaat masala and lemon juice to the chickpea masala.

4 Warm up the rotis/parathas in the microwave or in a dry frying pan/skillet.

5 To assemble, load up the rotis/parathas with the chickpea masala and top with your favourite sauces and salads and a drizzle of yogurt.

Crispy Five-Spice Chickpeas

These moreish little bites are a great snack to serve with drinks and they are fantastic sprinkled over a salad as a crunchy topping. They are made with the classic Bengali spice blend, panch phoron, which is easily sourced in Asian grocers or the spice aisle of larger supermarkets. Panch phoron is an aromatic blend of five whole spices – fenugreek, cumin, nigella, fennel and black mustard seeds – and brings a lovely crunch to this dish as well as a punchy flavour.

SERVES 3–4 AS A SNACK

400g/14oz canned chickpeas/
   garbanzo beans
1 tbsp tomato purée/paste

2 tbsp vegetable or sunflower oil
1 tbsp panch phoron spice mix
1 tsp salt
pinch of sugar

1 Preheat the oven to 160°C/320°F/gas mark 2 and line a baking sheet with non-stick baking parchment.

2 Drain the chickpeas and dry them thoroughly with a dish towel.

3 In a bowl, combine the drained chickpeas with the tomato purée, oil, panch phoron, salt and sugar, then mix really well.

4 Tumble the spiced chickpeas onto the prepared baking sheet and roast in the oven for 30–35 minutes, stirring every 10 minutes, or until crispy.

5 Leave to cool slightly before enjoying.

Cumin Green Beans

A delicious accompaniment to any curry, this is a simple, throw-together dish. Cumin is the signature note here, but you can play with other spice combinations, such as substituting the cumin seeds for panch phoron, or mustard seeds for a nuttier flavour.

SERVES 4

4 tbsp vegetable oil

2 tsp cumin seeds

1 brown onion, finely sliced

300g/10½oz green beans, topped, tailed and cut in half

¼ tsp ground turmeric

¼ tsp chilli powder

½ tsp ground cumin

2 tbsp chopped tomatoes

1½ tsp salt

1½ tsp sugar

1 Heat 3 tbsp of the oil in a wide non-stick frying pan/skillet that has a lid over a medium heat. When hot, add the cumin seeds and cook until dark brown, then add the onion and cook for 6–8 minutes, or until softened.

2 Heat the remaining 1 tbsp of oil in a separate pan over a medium heat. Add the green beans and fry for 2–3 minutes, then add the spiced onion mixture, ground spices, chopped tomatoes, salt and sugar along with a splash of water, cover and cook for a further 5–6 minutes, or until the green beans are cooked through with a little bite remaining.

3 Serve immediately.

Indian Mushy Peas

These Indian-inspired mushy peas are not spicy, but are instead sweetened with coconut. They make a good side dish for a curry-based sharing feast, but they go particularly well with my Halloumi Pakora (page 174) and chips/fries for a vegetarian take on British fish and chips.

SERVES 4

200g/7oz/1¼ cups frozen peas

50g/2oz unsalted butter

50g/2oz/½ cup desiccated/dried shredded coconut

grated zest and juice of ½ lime

2 tsp salt, or to taste

1 tsp sugar

small bunch of fresh mint, leaves only, finely chopped

1 Add the peas to a medium saucepan of boiling water and cook for 3–4 minutes, or until softened, then drain and set aside.

2 Return the pan to a medium-low heat, add the butter and let it melt, then add the desiccated coconut and cook, stirring, until toasted.

3 When the coconut is toasted, add the cooked peas along with the lime zest and juice, salt, sugar and the chopped mint. Stir to combine before roughly mashing together with a fork or potato masher.

4 Serve immediately.

Butter Bean & Piquillo Pepper Korma

Butter/lima beans are a wonderfully versatile ingredient in a vegetarian curry – their denser, heavier texture give the dish good structure. And I realize that it might sound like an unusual combination, but I have found that the Spanish piquillo pepper makes a fabulous addition to this mellow bean-based korma, giving it a little sweet, fruity lift. The crème fraîche that I use instead of the traditional cream also gives this a lighter, tangier flavour.

SERVES 4

3 tbsp vegetable oil

2 brown onions, roughly chopped

2 garlic cloves, finely chopped

5cm/2in piece of fresh ginger, peeled
 and finely chopped

2 tbsp garam masala

¼ tsp chilli powder

1 tsp ground turmeric

1½ tsp salt, or to taste

1½ tsp sugar

2 x 400g/14oz cans of butter/lima beans,
 drained and rinsed

50g/2oz/½ cup ground almonds

200ml/7fl oz/scant 1 cup water,
 or as needed

150g/5oz piquillo peppers, drained and
 roughly chopped

100ml/3½fl oz/scant ½ cup crème fraîche

handful of fresh coriander/cilantro, leaves
 and stems roughly chopped

1 Heat the oil in a medium saucepan that has a lid over a medium heat. When hot, add the onions and cook for 7–8 minutes, or until golden brown. Add the garlic and ginger, stir for 2 minutes, or until fragrant, then add the spices, salt and sugar.

2 Add the butter beans, ground almonds and measured water. Bring to a simmer, then cover the pan with the lid and cook for 6–8 minutes, or until the butter beans are cooked through but still with a little bite.

3 Stir through the piquillo peppers and crème fraîche. Taste for seasoning and add a splash more water if the curry looks too thick. Garnish with the chopped coriander and serve.

Green Mung Bean & Coconut Dal

I love green mung beans as they are powerhouses of goodness. This is the kind of food that is eaten day-in, day-out in India and for good reason – it's inexpensive, highly nutritious and easy to cook. The creamy sweetness lent by the coconut milk and the bright zing of the ginger will make this a must-have in your meat-free repertoire.

SERVES 2

250g/9oz/1¼ cups green mung beans

1.5 litres/52fl oz/6½ cups water

2 tsp salt

4 tbsp vegetable oil

2 tsp cumin seeds

1 tsp mustard seeds

2 bay leaves

2 dried red chillies

½ tsp asafoetida/hing

5cm/2in piece of fresh ginger, peeled and finely chopped

3 garlic cloves, finely chopped

1 tsp ground turmeric

2 tsp ground cumin

1 tsp sugar

1 x 400g/14oz can of chopped tomatoes

1 x 400ml/14fl oz can of coconut milk

large handful of fresh coriander/cilantro, leaves and stalks roughly chopped

1 Combine the green mung beans and measured water in a large saucepan and add 1 tsp of the salt. Bring to the boil, then reduce to a simmer and cook for 30–40 minutes, or until tender. Remove from the heat and set aside.

2 Heat the oil in a large non-stick saucepan over a medium heat. When hot, add the cumin and mustard seeds, and cook until dark brown. Add the bay leaves and dried red chillies, let sizzle a little, then add the asafoetida and stir for 30 seconds.

3 Add the ginger and garlic, and cook for 2–3 minutes, or until starting to soften, then add the turmeric and ground cumin along with the sugar and the remaining 1 tsp salt. Add the chopped tomatoes and cook for 5–6 minutes, or until starting to thicken.

4 Add the cooked mung beans to the pan along with the coconut milk and chopped coriander (keeping back a handful of coriander for garnish). Bring to the boil, then reduce to a simmer and cook for a final 6–8 minutes, or until you have a runny porridge consistency.

5 Serve, garnished with the remaining chopped coriander.

Preserved Lemon Masoor Dal

You might be familiar with adding preserved lemons to Moroccan dishes, such as tagines, but have you ever thought about adding them to a curry?! Preserved lemons have been pickled in salt – they taste lemony, yes, but it is a mellow rather than a sharp taste, and the peels and flesh become smooth and soft. They are the perfect addition to an earthy red lentil dal, lifting it to new heights.

SERVES 4

250g/9oz/1 cup red lentils

200g/7oz tomatoes, chopped

1 tsp salt

1 tsp ground turmeric

3 tbsp vegetable oil

3 tsp cumin seeds

2 tsp mustard seeds

1 large red chilli, finely sliced

½ tsp asafoetida/hing

¼ tsp chilli powder

1 tsp caster/superfine sugar

40g/1½oz preserved lemon, seeds
removed and fruit finely chopped

small bunch of fresh coriander/cilantro,
stems and leaves roughly chopped

1 Combine the red lentils, chopped tomatoes, salt and turmeric in a medium saucepan and cover with water. Bring to the boil, then reduce to a simmer and cook for 25–30 minutes, or until soft. Remove from the heat and set aside.

2 Heat a non-stick frying pan/skillet over a medium heat and add the oil. When hot, add the cumin seeds and cook until dark brown, then add the mustard seeds and red chilli. Cook until sizzling, then stir in the asafoetida and chilli powder.

3 Return the lentil pan to a medium heat, stir in the sugar, then pour in the tempered spices. Simmer for 5–6 minutes, or until the mixture is the consistency of thick porridge, then stir in the chopped preserved lemon.

4 Taste for seasoning, then serve, garnished with the chopped coriander.

Black Dal

This sumptuous dal always feels like such a treat. It is one of those special dishes where the simplest, humblest ingredients combine to form some kind of heavenly miracle. And the black gram lentils are so very nutritious. Make sure you buy whole lentils and not the split kind. It matters. This is best made with a pressure cooker, but you can cook it in a regular saucepan – it will just take longer.

SERVES 4

For the lentils
250g/9oz/1 cup whole black urad dal
1 x 400g/14oz can of chopped tomatoes
¼ tsp ground turmeric
½ tsp salt
1.25l/44fl oz/5¼ cups water

For the temper
2 tbsp vegetable oil
1 tsp cumin seeds
2 brown onions, finely chopped
4 garlic cloves, finely chopped

5cm/2in piece of fresh ginger, peeled
  and finely chopped
small bunch of fresh coriander/cilantro,
  leaves and stalks finely chopped
¼ tsp ground turmeric
¼ tsp chilli powder
2 tbsp garam masala
½ tsp salt
1 tsp sugar

To finish
juice of ½ lemon

1 Ideally, pressure cook the black urad dal with the chopped tomatoes, turmeric, salt and measured water until tender (according to the manufacturer's instructions). If you don't have a pressure cooker, add the same ingredients to a saucepan and simmer for 1 hour–1 hour 30 minutes, or until the lentils are tender.

2 Meanwhile, make the temper. Heat the oil in a non-stick frying pan/skillet over a medium–low heat. When hot, add the cumin seeds and let sizzle briefly, then add the onions, garlic, ginger and chopped coriander stalks (reserve the leaves for garnish), and cook for 6–8 minutes, or until everything is starting to soften. Add the turmeric, chilli powder, garam masala, salt and sugar, and cook for a further minute, or until fragrant.

3 When the lentils are cooked, pour the temper into the lentil pan along with the lemon juice and stir to combine.

4 Serve garnished with the chopped coriander leaves.

Yellow Dal with Beetroot Leaves

This dal made with yellow split peas is one that my family loves. It's so easy! I often cook the lentils in a pressure cooker initially to save time, but if you don't have one the method below in a regular saucepan works just as well. The beet leaves can be swapped for other greens such as baby spinach, radish tops or even baby radishes. The spice level is quite gentle – the chilli fiends among you can really ratchet up the heat by chopping rather than piercing the green chillies when adding to the temper, but that is up to you, of course!

SERVES 4

250g/9oz/1 cup yellow split lentils
   (toor dal)
¼ tsp ground turmeric
2 tsp salt
900ml/30fl oz/3½ cups water,
   or more as needed
3 tbsp vegetable oil

1 tsp cumin seeds
1 green chilli, pierced
½ tsp asafoetida/hing
¼ tsp chilli powder
leaves from 1 bunch of beetroot/beets,
   washed and roughly chopped
1½ tsp sugar
juice of ½ lemon

1 Combine the lentils, turmeric, 1 tsp of the salt and the measured water in a large saucepan and bring to the boil, then reduce to a simmer and cook for 30–40 minutes, or until the lentils are tender.

2 Meanwhile, heat the oil in a frying pan/skillet over a medium heat. When hot, add the cumin seeds and let them sizzle until they are a nice deep brown, then add the green chilli, asafoetida and chilli powder. Stir for a minute or so until fragrant. This mixture is called the temper.

3 Add the chopped beetroot leaves to the temper and let wilt briefly.

4 When the lentils are cooked, pour in the beetroot leaf temper, increase the heat to medium, and add the remaining 1 tsp salt, along with the sugar and lemon juice. Add a splash more water, if needed, and simmer to your preferred consistency. Ideally, the dal should be the consistency of thick porridge.

5 Taste for seasoning and serve.

Kidney Bean & Apricot Dopiaza

Kidney beans are a well-used ingredient in India, their dense texture taking on some of the characteristics of meat in vegetarian dishes. Here, they do the heavy lifting to bulk out this *dopiaza* and, although it might sound like an unusual pairing, go amazingly well with the fruity dried apricots. *Dopiaza* means "double onions" and it is the extra helping of crispy fried onions added at the end of cooking that make the dish so perennially popular.

SERVES 2, OR 4 AS PART OF A SHARING FEAST

4 tbsp vegetable oil

4 brown onions: 2 finely sliced; 2 finely chopped

1½ tsp salt

1 green chilli, pierced

5cm/2in piece of fresh ginger, peeled and finely chopped

3 garlic cloves, finely chopped

small bunch of fresh coriander/cilantro, leaves and stalks roughly chopped

1 tsp dried fenugreek leaves (kasuri methi)

1 tsp ground turmeric

½ tsp chilli powder

2 tsp garam masala

1 tbsp ground cumin

1 tsp freshly ground black pepper

1 tbsp tomato purée/paste

1 x 400g/14oz can of kidney beans, drained and rinsed

30g/1oz dried apricots, finely chopped

1 tsp sugar

150–200ml/5–7fl oz/⅔–scant 1 cup just-boiled water

naan breads and chutneys of choice, to serve

1 Heat 2 tbsp of the oil in a wide non-stick frying pan/skillet over a medium heat. When hot, add the sliced onions with ½ tsp of the salt and cook, stirring, for 10–15 minutes, or until very soft and caramelized.

2 Meanwhile, heat the remaining 2 tbsp of oil in a medium saucepan that has a lid over a medium heat. When hot, add the green chilli and sizzle for 1 minute, then add the chopped onions and cook for 7–8 minutes, or until golden brown. Add the ginger, garlic, green chilli, chopped coriander stalks (reserving the leaves for garnish) and the dried fenugreek leaves, and cook for 4 minutes, stirring, until everything is starting to soften.

3 Add the spices to the saucepan, stir well, then add the tomato purée. Cook for another 2–3 minutes, or until fragrant, then add the drained kidney beans, dried apricots, sugar and the remaining 1 tsp of salt. Stir to combine, then pour in 150ml/5fl oz/⅔ cup of the water. Bring to the boil, then reduce to a simmer, cover and cook for 8–10 minutes, or until the kidney beans are cooked through. Check the water level, adding more if it gets too dry.

4 Finally, stir through the caramelized sliced onions. Garnish with the chopped coriander leaves just before serving. Serve with naan breads and chutneys, as desired.

Broad Bean Stuffed Puris

These are not an everyday bread – we eat puris when we want a treat. They are the breads of celebration in my family, cooked up for parties and *puja* festivals. A spiced broad/fava bean filling gives them an extra layer of deliciousness. Traditionally fried in ghee, I've used vegetable oil for convenience, as well as frozen beans (by all means, substitute freshly podded beans when they are in season, if you have the time to prepare them). Enjoy these stuffed puris as an alternative to other breads, such as naans or chapatis, when eating a saucier curry.

MAKES 6

For the filling
100g/3½oz/scant 1 cup frozen broad/
    fava beans
2.5cm/1in piece of fresh ginger, peeled
    and roughly chopped
1 green chilli, finely chopped
juice of ½ lemon
1 tsp garam masala
½ tsp amchur/mango powder

1 tsp ground cumin
1 tsp salt

For the dough
200g/7oz/scant 2 cups chapati flour (atta),
    plus extra for dusting
2 tsp vegetable oil, plus extra for cooking
3½ tsp salt
80–100ml/3–3½fl oz/⅓–scant ½ cup water

1 Bring a saucepan of water to the boil, add the broad beans and simmer for 6–8 minutes, or until starting to soften, then drain well.

2 Transfer the beans to a food processor along with the ginger, green chilli and lemon juice and blitz until roughly chopped. Stir in the spices and salt. Tip out onto a plate and divide into 6 balls of equal size. Set aside.

3 Meanwhile, make the dough. Place the chapati flour in a mixing bowl, add the oil and salt, then slowly pour in the measured water, stirring with a wooden spoon until a dough forms. Knead for 4–5 minutes until smooth, then divide into 6 balls of equal size.

4 Take one dough ball, and roll it out on a lightly floured surface to a 12cm/5in circle. Place a ball of the broad bean paste in the middle, then wrap the dough around it to form a round parcel until fully enclosed. Press down lightly, then roll out again to a similar-size circle. Repeat with the remaining dough balls and broad bean paste.

5 Heat a little oil in a non-stick frying pan/skillet over a medium–high heat. When hot, add the first puri and cook for 3–4 minutes on each side, or until browned and starting to crisp up a little. Remove to a plate and repeat with remaining puris.

5

BRASSICAS & LEAFY GREENS

Brassicas, such as broccoli, kale, kohlrabi, cauliflower and Brussels sprouts, are very useful in the Indian kitchen, lending themselves to salads as much as hot dishes, and can work well with pretty much any spicing you want to try. I've put them together with the lovely leafy greens – spinach, cabbage, chard – as they are equally amenable. I hope you find some nice new ideas for using them in this chapter.

Broccoli & Coconut Bhajis

Who says bhajis have to be made of onion? Bhajis are a great vehicle for any kind of veg – have a look at your fridge leftovers and get creative! These battered broccoli and coconut bites are right up my street. With a hint of mustard seed and garlic (the magic brassica combo) and a bit of texture from the coconut, they make a perfect change-up to your traditional curry starter. Don't forget a dipping chutney or raita …

SERVES 4

vegetable oil, for deep-frying

260g/9½oz/2⅓ cups gram flour/besan

¼ tsp bicarbonate of soda/baking soda

1 tsp ajwain seeds

1 tsp mustard seeds

2 garlic cloves, crushed

15 curry leaves, finely sliced

2 tsp ground coriander

2 tsp ground cumin

¼ tsp chilli powder

2 tsp salt

300ml/10½fl oz/1¼ cups sparkling water

juice of 1 lemon

200g/7oz broccoli, stems and florets cut into
bite-size pieces

30g/1oz/½ cup dried coconut flakes/chips

2 tbsp chopped fresh coriander/cilantro

your favourite chutney or raita, to serve

1 Heat a 5cm/2in depth of oil in a deep, heavy-based saucepan or deep-fat fryer to 180°C/350°F. You'll know it's hot enough when you can add a piece of bread or a sprinkling of flour and it sizzles and floats to the surface.

2 Meanwhile, add the flour, bicarbonate of soda, ajwain and mustard seeds, crushed garlic, curry leaves, ground spices, chilli powder and salt to a large bowl and stir to combine. Pour in the sparkling water and whisk to a smooth batter the consistency of single/pouring cream. Add the lemon juice and whisk again to combine.

3 Add the broccoli, dried coconut and coriander to the bowl and stir to coat everything in the batter.

4 Carefully drop tablespoonfuls of the bhaji mixture into the hot oil in batches and cook for 2 minutes until golden, then turn and cook on the other side for a further 2 minutes. Remove with a slotted spoon to a plate lined with paper towels to absorb excess oil. Repeat until all the mixture is used up.

5 Serve hot with chutney or raita for dipping.

Samosa Tart

This takes the cauliflower-based filling of *shingara* (the Bengali version of samosas) and uses it as the topping for an accessible tart using puff pastry. It makes great party food or a light lunch. You can also alter the filling to suit your taste or whatever fresh veg you have in the fridge – chopped bell peppers, broccoli, leeks or squash would also work well here, as would green chillies in place of the red for a different flavour dimension.

SERVES 4

- 2 tbsp vegetable oil
- 2 tsp panch phoron
- 1 red onion, finely chopped
- 2.5cm/1 in piece of fresh ginger, peeled and finely chopped
- 150g/5oz cauliflower, chopped into small bite-size pieces
- 100g/3½oz potato, peeled and chopped into 1cm/½in cubes
- ½ tsp ground turmeric
- 1 tsp salt
- ½ tsp sugar
- 100g/3½oz/⅔ cup frozen garden peas
- 1 x ready-rolled puff pastry sheet
- small bunch of fresh coriander/cilantro, stems and leaves finely chopped
- 1 red chilli, finely sliced
- milk, for brushing

1 Heat the oil in a medium non-stick saucepan that has a lid over a medium heat. When hot, add the panch phoron and cook until the nuggets of fenugreek turn dark brown. Be careful not to burn, as it will taste bitter. Add the onions and cook until softened, then stir in the ginger.

2 Add the chopped cauliflower and potato and stir to combine, then add the turmeric, salt and sugar. Add a splash of water, then cover with a lid and cook for 4–5 minutes, or until the vegetables have softened.

3 Stir in the peas, remove from the heat and leave until the mixture is completely cool.

4 Meanwhile, preheat the oven to 200°C/400°F/gas mark 6.

5 Unroll the pastry sheet and place on a lined baking sheet (you can use the paper the pastry came wrapped in for lining the sheet). Spread the cooled filling mixture over the surface of the pastry sheet, leaving a gap of about 2.5cm/1in around the edges. Sprinkle over the coriander and red chilli. To create a pretty effect, score the edges of the pastry sheet and brush with a little milk.

6 Bake for 20–25 minutes, or until the pastry is golden brown and crispy all over.

7 Serve on its own or with a side salad.

One-Bowl Superfood Salad

A festival of colour and flavour, this kale salad is life-changing – I can't get enough of it and eat it almost every day. If you have leftovers, they last for about 3 days in the fridge (the apple cider vinegar stops the apples from turning brown). Packed with nutrients, the zingy apple, fennel and goji berries lift it to another dimension and the dressing is to die for. With toasty crunch from the nuts and seeds, I can't think of anything better.

SERVES 4–6

50g/2oz/¼ cup quinoa
50g/2oz/⅓ cup cashew nuts
30g/1oz/¼ cup pumpkin seeds
2 large handfuls of kale, stalks removed,
    leaves torn (prepared weight about
    200g/7oz)
juice of ½ lemon
1 tsp salt
1 small fennel bulb, tough core removed,
    very finely sliced
1 red apple, cored and roughly chopped

1 carrot, peeled and grated or julienned
30g/1oz/¼ cup goji berries
handful of fresh coriander/cilantro, stalks
    and leaves roughly chopped

For the dressing

6 tbsp sesame oil
1 red chilli, chopped
3 tsp maple syrup
3 tbsp apple cider vinegar
salt, to taste

1 Cook the quinoa according to the packet instructions, then drain and rinse well under cold running water.

2 Meanwhile, heat a small non-stick frying pan/skillet over a medium heat. When hot, add the cashews and pumpkin seeds and toast for 3–4 minutes, taking care not to let them burn. Remove and set aside.

3 Return the pan to a low heat, add the sesame oil for the dressing, then add the chopped red chilli. Cook until sizzling, then pour into a bowl and set aside to cool.

4 Briefly blanch the kale in boiling water until softened slightly, then drain. In a large mixing bowl, combine the kale with the lemon juice and salt. Add the fennel, apple, carrot, goji berries, coriander and drained quinoa. Mix until well combined.

5 Add the rest of the dressing ingredients to the bowl with the cooled sesame oil and mix together. Taste for seasoning.

6 Pour the dressing over the salad and toss through. Serve garnished with the toasted cashews and pumpkin seeds.

Kohrabi & Radish Salad

Kohlrabi is a brassica in the mustard family and I've found it to be rather an underrated ingredient outside of India, but it's wonderful in so many dishes. The flesh tastes rather like broccoli, but a little sweeter and milder. It's great in curries, but I also love it finely sliced and used in a fresh salad or a slaw. This salad is sweet and peppery and ideal for a late summer lunch.

SERVES 4

1 small kohlrabi (about 250g/9oz peeled weight), cut into thin batons

½ cucumber, chopped into thin batons

100g/3½oz radishes, quartered

2 spring onions/scallions, sliced on the diagonal

grated zest of 1 lime and the juice of ½ lime

1 tsp ground cumin

2 tsp smoked salt

1 tsp black pepper

½ tsp sugar

1 In a mixing bowl, mix together the kohlrabi and cucumber batons, quartered radishes and sliced spring onions.

2 Add the lime zest and juice, then add the cumin, smoked salt, black pepper and sugar.

3 Taste to check you have the balance of seasoning just right, then serve.

Indian Green Chopped Salad

This spicy little side salad, full of gorgeous greens, goes with just about all the curries in this book and makes a great filling for the Chickpea Kati Rolls (page 92).

SERVES 4–6

2 celery stalks, finely chopped

100g/3½oz lettuce, finely chopped

2 long Turkish chillies, finely sliced

1 avocado, peeled, pitted and finely chopped

½ fennel bulb, finely chopped

2 spring onions/scallions, finely sliced

small bunch of fresh coriander/cilantro, stems only, finely chopped (use the leaves in the dressing)

1 red chilli, finely chopped, to garnish (optional)

For the dressing

100g/3½oz/⅔ cup cashew nuts

1 banana shallot, peeled and roughly chopped

juice of 1 lemon

leaves of 1 small bunch of coriander/ cilantro (see left)

50g/2oz baby spinach, washed

½ tsp mustard paste

1 tsp sugar

2 tbsp vegetable oil

1 tbsp mustard oil

1 tsp salt

5 tbsp water, or as needed

1 Start with the dressing. Place the cashews in a bowl and pour over enough boiling water to cover. Leave to soak and soften for 15 minutes.

2 Drain the cashews, then add to a food processor with the remaining dressing ingredients. Blitz to combine to a paste, adding more water if needed.

3 Combine all the vegetables in a large mixing bowl. Add the dressing and mix until well combined, adding a little more water again if the dressing needs loosening.

4 Taste for seasoning before serving sprinkled with red chilli, if using.

Gunpowder Florets

This recipe comes out with all guns blazing, livening up cauliflower and broccoli florets with my signature spiced batter. Once you start popping these little bites, it's very hard to stop, so make sure you've got enough to go around! Serve with your favourite chutneys, for dipping.

SERVES 4 AS A SHARING STARTER

½ small cauliflower (about 300g/10½oz), chopped into small florets

200g/7oz broccoli, chopped into small florets

2 garlic cloves, finely chopped or grated

2.5cm/1in piece of fresh ginger, peeled and finely chopped or grated

1 tsp salt

¼ tsp chilli powder

½ tsp ground turmeric

2 tsp ground cumin

2 tsp ground coriander

4 eggs, beaten

200g/7oz/1¾ cups gram flour/besan

vegetable oil, for deep-frying

To garnish (optional)

2 spring onions/scallions, finely sliced

2 red chillies, finely sliced

small bunch of fresh coriander/cilantro, leaves and stems finely chopped

1 tsp chaat masala

1 In a large bowl, combine the cauliflower, broccoli, garlic, ginger, salt and spices. Set aside to marinate for 15 minutes.

2 After 15 minutes, add the beaten egg to the bowl and toss to combine, then add the gram flour and mix until the cauliflower and broccoli pieces are well coated.

3 Heat a 5cm/2in depth of oil in a deep-fat fryer or heavy-based saucepan to 180°C/350°F. You'll know it's hot enough when you can drizzle in 1 tsp of batter and it floats to the surface.

4 Fry the coated cauliflower and broccoli in the hot oil in batches for 3–4 minutes, or until crispy and golden brown. Remove with a slotted spoon to drain on paper towels.

5 Arrange in a serving dish and garnish with the spring onions, chillies and coriander, if using. Sprinkle over the chaat masala and serve.

Spinach & Portobello Curry

This iron-rich spinach curry is bolstered by the portobello mushrooms – they are a classic combination. This is a simple, saucy curry that is great for a midweek supper. Cooking the mushrooms and spinach separately from the sauce means they don't go all mushy and you get great texture and flavour from the finished dish.

SERVES 4

2 tbsp vegetable oil

5 dried curry leaves

2 red onions, roughly chopped

3 garlic cloves, crushed

5cm/2in piece of fresh ginger, peeled
  and finely chopped

1 tsp ground turmeric

¼ tsp chilli powder

1 tbsp ground cumin

2 tbsp ground coriander

1½ tsp salt

1 x 400g/14oz can of chopped tomatoes

1 tbsp tomato purée/paste

200ml/7fl oz/scant 1 cup water

500g/1lb 2oz portobello mushrooms,
  roughly chopped

400g/14oz spinach

1 tsp garam masala

small bunch of fresh coriander/cilantro,
  finely chopped

1 Heat the oil in a large, wide-based pan over a medium heat. When hot, add the curry leaves and let them sizzle, then add the onions and cook for 5–6 minutes, or until softened and starting to brown.

2 Add the garlic and ginger and cook for 3–4 minutes, or until fragrant, then add the spices, salt, chopped tomatoes and tomato purée. Stir for a minute, then add the measured water and cook for 5–6 minutes, or until starting to thicken. Remove from the heat and set aside to cool.

3 When the mixture is cool, blitz it in a food processor or using a hand-held blender until smooth.

4 Wipe out the pan with paper towels, then reheat over a high heat until very hot. Dry-fry the mushrooms until starting to colour, then add the spinach and let it wilt. Reduce the heat, then add the blended sauce along with the garam masala and simmer for a further 4–5 minutes, or until the mushrooms are cooked through.

5 Stir through the chopped coriander and enjoy.

Cabbage Curry

An easy curry that pays homage to a veg that is revered in the Eastern kitchen, far more than in the Western one – the simple white cabbage. Spice brings this humble veg to life. This, with a little slick of ghee at the end to bring it round to a luxurious finish, makes a wonderful supper dish.

SERVES 4

2 tbsp vegetable oil

2 bay leaves

1 tbsp cumin seeds

100g/3½oz potatoes, peeled and chopped into small bite-size pieces

100g/3½oz/⅔ cup peas

100ml/3½fl oz/scant ½ cup water

1 tsp ground turmeric

½ tsp ground coriander

¼ tsp chilli powder

3 tbsp chopped tomatoes

300g/10½oz white cabbage, shredded and rinsed

1 tsp salt

1 tsp sugar

juice of ½ lemon

2 tbsp ghee

1 Heat the oil in a wide pan that has a lid over a medium heat. When hot, add the bay leaves and cumin seeds and let sizzle briefly, then add the potatoes, peas and measured water. Cover and cook for 10–12 minutes, or until the potatoes are softening.

2 When the potatoes are half cooked, add the ground spices, chilli powder and chopped tomatoes, and stir until well combined.

3 Add the shredded cabbage, salt and sugar, and cook, covered, for 6–8 minutes, or until all the veg is cooked through.

4 Stir in the lemon juice and ghee just before serving.

Rainbow Chard Chorchuri

Chorchuri is a Bengali dry dish of mixed vegetables, often involving lots of root veg or gourds, but really it is one of those versatile medley dishes in which you can chop and change for whatever is in season. I love this rainbow chard version as it's so colourful, but if you can't find the chard, swap for spinach, which is added at the end when you would add the reserved chard leaves to wilt in the pan. It can be served with a dal for a traditional touch, but plain white rice is the usual carb of choice.

SERVES 4

5 tbsp vegetable oil

1 tbsp panch phoron

2 dried red chillies

100g/3½oz rainbow chard, stems chopped and leaves set aside

200g/7oz white potato, peeled and chopped into small chunks

½ mooli/daikon, peeled and chopped into small chunks

1½ tsp salt

1 aubergine/eggplant, chopped into small chunks

1 tsp ground turmeric

½ tsp chilli powder

1 tsp sugar

½ tsp mustard paste

100ml/3½fl oz/scant ½ cup boiling water

1 Heat 3 tbsp of the oil in a wide pan that has a lid over a medium heat. When hot, add the panch phoron and dried red chillies and cook until the nuggets of fenugreek turn dark brown. Be careful not to burn, as it will taste bitter. Add the chopped chard stems, potato, mooli and salt, cover and cook for 8–10 minutes, or until softened, adding a splash of water if needed.

2 Add the remaining 2 tbsp of oil to the pan, then add the aubergine and cook for 2–3 minutes until starting to brown all over. Add the spices, sugar and mustard paste, then pour in the boiling water. Cover and cook for a final 5 minutes, or until all the vegetables are cooked through.

3 Stir through the reserved chard leaves right at the end and let wilt, then taste for seasoning before serving.

Angry Cauliflower

This is basically the Mowgli Angry Bird (the original recipe for which can be found in *Mowgli Street Food*), but plant-based. There's something luxurious about serving up a whole, roasted cauliflower that has drunk in the hot, spicy marinade to become soft and yielding, but fiery in colour and flavour. You could serve it with some turmeric-rubbed roast potatoes and my Indian Green Chopped Salad (page 122). It's also lovely served with a simple lemon-dressed green salad and a raita. If you wanted to make this an even more hearty dish, you could serve it on a bed of warm whole grains. It's very versatile, so make it your own.

SERVES 6–8

400g/14oz/generous 1½ cups
   Greek yogurt
1 tsp ground turmeric
½ tsp chilli powder
2 tsp ground cumin
2 tsp ground coriander
½ tsp ground cinnamon
1 tsp Kashmiri chilli powder
2 tbsp tandoori masala

5cm/2in piece of fresh ginger, peeled
   and finely chopped or grated
3 garlic cloves, finely chopped or grated
1½ tsp salt
juice of ½ lemon
2 tbsp vegetable oil
1 whole baby cauliflower (about 600g/
   1lb 5oz)
fresh green salad (or Indian Green Chopped
   Salad, page 122) and Spinach Raita
   (page 139), to serve

1 Add all the ingredients, except the cauliflower, to a large mixing bowl. Mix well and taste for seasoning.

2 Use a sharp knife to make deep cuts in the entire surface of the cauliflower. Add the cauliflower to the marinade and use your hands to rub the marinade all over. Cover, then leave to marinate in the refrigerator overnight.

3 When you're ready to cook, preheat the oven to 200°C/400°F/gas mark 6 and line a baking sheet with baking parchment.

4 Place the cauliflower on the baking sheet and roast it in the oven for 45 minutes–1 hour, or until cooked through. A sharp knife or skewer should easily go all the way through the cauliflower with no resistance.

5 Serve whole or slice up for your guests to enjoy with a green salad or raita.

Juniper Tangled Greens

Winter greens should never be boring. This is a new twist on my Calcutta Tangled Greens (the original recipe for which can be found in *Mowgli Street Food*), using the spiky freshness of juniper to liven up this essential cabbage side dish. Once you've tried it, you'll want to serve it with everything. *Pictured opposite with the Brussels Sprouts with Mustard Seeds (page 134).*

SERVES 4

3 tbsp vegetable oil

1 tbsp mustard seeds

3 garlic cloves, finely chopped

10 juniper berries, lightly crushed in a pestle
  and mortar or with the side of a heavy knife

½ tsp ground turmeric

1 sweetheart cabbage/hispi, core removed
  and finely shredded

1½ tsp salt

1 tsp sugar

juice of ½ lemon

1 Heat the oil in a large non-stick frying pan/skillet over a medium heat. When hot, add the mustard seeds and let sizzle until fragrant, then add the garlic and crushed juniper berries and cook for 3–4 minutes, or until fragrant.

2 Add the turmeric, stir, then add the shredded cabbage along with the salt and sugar. Cook for 5–6 minutes, or until the cabbage has wilted and cooked through.

3 Squeeze in the lemon juice and serve hot.

Brussels Sprouts with Mustard Seeds

Mustard seeds are quite a magical ingredient when used with any brassica, and Brussels sprouts are no exception. This is as simple as Indian vegetable cooking gets, with a classic spice trio of mustard seeds, chilli and turmeric. A squeeze of lemon juice at the end wouldn't go amiss either, if you like. *Pictured on page 133, top.*

SERVES 2–4 AS A SIDE

200g/7oz Brussels sprouts

1½ tsp salt

2 tbsp vegetable oil

2 tsp black mustard seeds

½ tsp chilli powder

1 tsp ground turmeric

1 tsp English mustard paste loosened
with a little water

1½ tsp sugar

squeeze of lemon juice

1 First, cook the Brussels sprouts. Tip the sprouts into a large pan, pour in about a 2cm/¾in depth of water and add ½ tsp of the salt. Cover and bring to the boil, then reduce to a simmer and cook with the lid on for 3–5 minutes, depending on size, or until they are tender to the point of a sharp knife. Drain, tip the sprouts into a bowl and set aside.

2 Heat the oil in a frying pan/skillet over a medium heat. When hot, add the mustard seeds and let sizzle until fragrant, then add the cooked Brussels sprouts along with the chilli powder, turmeric and mustard paste. Cook until fully warmed through (or for 3–4 minutes, if using previously cooked sprouts, until hot).

3 Stir through the remaining 1 tsp salt along with the sugar and lemon juice, and taste for seasoning before serving.

Emerald Fried Rice

This is an easy and interesting way to mix up your rice with some healthy greens. It is best made with pre-cooked rice, either made a few hours before or even the day before, but you can make the rice just before cooking the dish – just ensure it is fully cooled and drained before using. It is lovely served with Monsoon Mushroom Madras (page 205) or the Black Dal (page 104).

SERVES 2–3

200g/7oz baby spinach
3 garlic cloves, finely chopped
1 brown onion, finely chopped
juice of ½ lime

1 tbsp vegetable oil
2 tsp cumin seeds
generous pinch of salt
200g/7oz/generous 1 cup
cooked basmati rice

1 Add the baby spinach to a pan of boiling water and cook for 2 minutes, then drain and plunge into a bowl of iced water to stop the cooking process. Squeeze out all the water from the spinach.

2 Add the spinach to a high-speed blender along with the garlic, onion and lime juice and blitz to a purée.

3 Heat the oil in a wide pan over a medium heat. Add the cumin seeds and let them sizzle, then add the spinach purée along with a generous pinch of salt. Cook for 3–4 minutes, or until thickened, then add the cooked rice and stir through for a further 3–4 minutes until piping hot.

4 Taste for seasoning, then serve immediately.

Aromatic Cauliflower Rice

Sometimes you just want to cook a smaller meal and this recipe is exactly that. Super easy to make, it makes a meal for two in just one pan, but it can also be scaled up if needed. In the interest of speed and ease, I've used ready-made crispy onions – the cheat's way to those caramelized onions often found in Indian rice dishes. It is also unusual for me to use whole spices, but I find that for aromatic rice it's the only way to achieve a really deep flavour. This works very well enjoyed with a raita, such as the Spinach Raita (page 139).

SERVES 2

½ small head of cauliflower, chopped into small florets, stalks roughly chopped

2 tbsp vegetable oil

1 small cinnamon stick

2 Indian bay leaves

1 dried red chilli

2 cloves

30g/1oz/3 tbsp cashew nuts, roughly chopped

2.5cm/1in piece of fresh ginger, peeled and finely chopped or grated

1–2 green chillies, finely sliced

½ tsp ground turmeric

1 tsp ground coriander

1 tsp ground cumin

1 tsp garam masala

1 tbsp tomato purée/paste

200g/7 oz/1 cup basmati rice

2 handfuls of frozen peas

400ml/14fl oz/1⅔ cups water

juice of ½ lemon

30g/1oz/3 tbsp ready-made crispy onions

handful of fresh coriander/cilantro (roughly chopped, if wished)

salt, to taste

1 Add the cauliflower florets and stalks to a large pan of salted boiling water and cook for 5–6 minutes, or until tender but still holding their shape. Drain and set aside.

2 Heat the oil in a medium saucepan over a medium heat. When hot, add the cinnamon, bay leaves, dried red chilli and cloves, let sizzle for 30 seconds, then add the cashew nuts and stir.

3 Add the ginger, chillies, ground spices and tomato purée with a splash of water to bring it all together, then add the drained cauliflower with a generous pinch of salt and stir to coat in the spice paste.

4 Stir in the rice and peas, then add the measured water. Bring to the boil, then reduce to a simmer and cook for 10 minutes, or until all the water has been absorbed.

5 Squeeze in the lemon juice to finish and enjoy garnished with the crispy onions and coriander, either on its own or with some plain yogurt or raita.

Spinach Raita

This is a really easy and nutritious raita. Cooling and wholesome with some added greens, it's great for serving to kids and is ideal served alongside any spicy curry or as a dip for fried chops or bhajis.

SERVES 3–4

100g/3½oz baby spinach
200g/7oz/1 cup Greek yogurt
juice of ½ lemon

1 tsp salt
1 tsp vegetable oil
2 garlic cloves, finely sliced
½ tsp ground cumin

1 Add the baby spinach to a pan of boiling water and cook for 2 minutes, then drain and transfer to a bowl of iced water to stop the cooking process. Fully squeeze the water out of the spinach, then roughly chop.

2 Add the chopped spinach to a bowl, then mix in the Greek yogurt, lemon juice and salt.

3 Heat the oil in a small frying pan/skillet over a medium-low heat. When hot, add the sliced garlic and cook for 3–4 minutes, or until starting to crisp up, then stir in the ground cumin. Remove from the heat and let cool slightly.

4 Spoon the crispy spiced garlic over the spinach yogurt and enjoy!

Kale Superfood Smoothie

Packed with all the superfoods I love, this cleansing smoothie is ideal for giving you some get-up-and-go. The sweetness of the apple juice and the dates, plus the zing of lime and ginger, offsets the earthiness of the kale. I recommend you try it!

SERVES 2

4 ice cubes

2 large handfuls of kale (about 40g/1½oz)

½ avocado, peeled and pitted

5cm/2in piece of fresh ginger, peeled and finely chopped

3 Medjool dates, pitted

½ tsp ground cumin

½ tsp black salt (kala namak) (optional)

juice of ½ lime

100ml/3½fl oz/scant 1½ cups apple juice

200ml/7fl oz/scant 1 cup water, or more as needed

orange slices, to garnish

1 Add all the ingredients to a high-speed blender and blitz until smooth, adding a splash more water to get the consistency you like, if needed.

2 Divide between 2 glasses, garnish with orange slices and enjoy immediately.

6
FRUIT

Juicy, fresh, tantalizing ... the options for making the most of fruit in the Mowgli meat-free kitchen are exciting. As well as a spiced version of a fruit salad (honestly, fruit with spices is a taste sensation, so don't flick past it thinking it's a bit weird), and some delicious desserts and drinks, I've included a number of curry mains, as fruits work in savoury dishes just as beautifully.

Paneer, Cashew & Mango Curry

A fruity, nutty, creamy, sunshiney delight, this dish is a real lift to the senses. Make sure you get large, ripe mangoes for optimum flavour. Your summertime supper sorted! It is easily doubled to serve four.

SERVES 2

2 tbsp vegetable oil

½ tsp black mustard seeds

1 red onion, roughly chopped

2.5cm/1in piece of fresh ginger, peeled and finely chopped

2 garlic cloves, finely chopped or crushed

1 green chilli, finely chopped

2 tbsp garam masala

1 tsp ground coriander

1 tsp ground cumin

½ tsp ground turmeric

¼ tsp chilli powder

1 tsp salt

1 tsp sugar

225g/8oz paneer, chopped into small chunks

½ large mango, flesh diced into 1cm/½in pieces

50g/2oz/⅓ cup cashew nuts

50g/2oz/scant ¼ cup coconut cream

100ml/3½fl oz/scant ½ cup water, or as needed

lemon juice, to taste

handful of fresh coriander/cilantro, roughly chopped

1 Heat the oil in a large non-stick pan that has a lid over a medium heat. When hot, add the mustard seeds and let sizzle, then add the onion and cook for 5–6 minutes, or until starting to soften.

2 Add the chopped ginger, garlic and green chilli, cook for 2–3 minutes, then add the ground spices, chilli powder, salt and sugar.

3 Add the paneer and cook for 3–4 minutes, or until starting to colour all over, then add the diced mango, cashews, coconut cream and measured water. Cover with the pan lid and simmer for 6–8 minutes, or until the paneer is cooked through, adding a splash more water if needed.

4 Season with lemon juice and garnish with the chopped coriander before serving.

Jackfruit & Apricot Biryani

A wonderful aromatic biryani is a real showstopper dish – no Indian celebration is complete without one. I love lifting the lid and letting the perfumed steam escape, then delving into those colourful layers of goodness, with caramelized onions and pillowy soft golden saffron rice – is there a better centrepiece dish out there? Jackfruit is a fairly recent addition to the Western diet, its popularity increasing as the search for vegan and vegetarian meat substitutes has marched on, but it has been enjoyed in India since ancient times. This recipe makes the most of the jackfruit's fibrous unripe flesh. A fruity number that can't fail to impress.

SERVES 4

5 tbsp vegetable oil

2 large onions, finely diced

4 garlic cloves, crushed

5cm/2in piece of fresh ginger, peeled and crushed

600g/1lb 5oz canned jackfruit, drained and chopped

1 tsp ground turmeric

¼ tsp chilli powder

3 tbsp garam masala

1 cinnamon stick

2 cloves

3 green cardamom pods

2 tsp salt

1 tsp sugar

50g/1¾oz dried apricots, finely diced

375ml/13fl oz/2 cups water

For the rice

600ml/20fl oz/2½ cups cold water

400g/14oz/1½ cups white basmati rice

2 tsp salt

1 tsp ground turmeric

For the saffron milk

1 tsp saffron strands

100ml/3½fl oz/scant ½ cup warm milk

For the onions

3 large onions, finely sliced

5 tbsp vegetable oil

1 tsp salt

For the dough seal

120g/4oz/1 cup plain/all-purpose or chapati flour

3 tbsp water

2 tsp vegetable oil

To garnish

pomegranate seeds

chopped fresh coriander/cilantro

Method overleaf

1 Set a large wok that has a lid over a medium heat. Add the oil, onions, ginger and garlic, and fry until golden brown. Add the jackfruit and cook for 2–3 minutes, then add all the spices, salt, sugar and apricots and stir-fry for 3 minutes. Add the measured water, cover and simmer over a medium–low heat for 25 minutes.

2 Meanwhile, make the rice. Combine the measured water, rice, salt and turmeric in a large pan and simmer over a medium-low heat for about 8 minutes until the rice has just absorbed the water. Cover and set aside.

3 In a small bowl, steep the saffron strands in the warm milk for 20 minutes.

4 In a separate pan, gently fry the onions in the oil until golden, then remove with a slotted spoon to a plate lined with paper towels and season with the salt.

5 Preheat the oven to 200°C/400°F/gas mark 6.

6 Spoon a layer of the rice into a large ovenproof dish. Cover with half of the fried onions, then add another thin layer of rice. Add half of the jackfruit curry, then add another layer of rice, then the remaining onions and another layer of rice. Top with the remaining curry, then add a final layer of rice. Pour the saffron milk over the top of the rice. Cover the dish with the lid.

7 Mix the ingredients for the dough seal together in a bowl. Create a long sausage of dough and seal the join between the lid and the dish so no steam can escape.

8 Bake for 35 minutes.

9 At the end of the cooking time, remove the dish from the oven, break the dough seal at the table for a bit of drama and serve portions of the biryani garnished with a scattering of pomegranate seeds and coriander.

Aunty Mona's Green Mango Chutney

This is one of my favourite chutneys and my Aunty Mona's recipe really can't be beaten. It is so eye-wateringly good, you'll be looking for excuses to serve it with everything. You must get green unripe mangoes for this – you'll find them in Asian shops and they are quite hard and white-fleshed inside. The pungent punch of mustard oil is key, too. It may look like you use a lot of sugar, but you need it to balance the sharpness of the green mango. It pairs with curry and rice as it does with bhajis or pakoras or samosas … honestly, with everything! *Pictured on page 151, left.*

**MAKES 1 SMALL JAR
   (ABOUT 4 SERVINGS)**
2 green mangoes, peeled and flesh
   roughly chopped

2 green chillies
1 tsp salt, or more as needed
5 tbsp sugar, or as needed
4 tbsp mustard oil

1 Place the green mango flesh in a food processor along with the green chillies and blitz until roughly chopped.

2 Transfer to a mixing bowl, add the salt and half of the sugar and stir to combine. Stir through the mustard oil, then taste for seasoning. It should be well balanced, so add more sugar if needed.

3 Store in a sterilized jar in the refrigerator for up to 4 days.

Gooseberry Chutney

I've given you a few chutney recipes in this book, because, honestly, they are the most wonderful thing to make when you need to use up the seasonal gluts of fruits and vegetables. Sitting quietly on your refrigerator shelf, getting better with time and livening up any meal they are added to, I can't resist them. In India, amla – gooseberries – are revered for their health-giving properties and are considered a sacred fruit by Hindus. *Amla chutney* is a spicy, jammy concoction that goes very nicely with poppadoms or with spicy curries. *Pictured right with Aunty Mona's Green Mango Chutney (page 149).*

MAKES 300G/10½OZ/1 CUP (4 SERVINGS)

1 x 300g/10½oz can of gooseberries
   in syrup
1 tbsp vegetable oil
1 tsp cumin seeds
1 tsp fennel seeds
1 tsp mustard seeds
¼ tsp chilli powder
1 tsp ground turmeric
1 tsp salt
40–50g/1½–2oz/¼–⅓ cup
   soft brown sugar
juice of ½ lemon

1 Drain the canned gooseberries, reserving 3 tbsp of the syrup.

2 Heat the oil in a small saucepan over a medium heat. When hot, add the cumin seeds, fennel seeds and mustard seeds and let sizzle until dark brown.

3 Add the chilli powder, turmeric and salt, then add the sugar, lemon juice, gooseberries and the reserved syrup. Simmer for 5 minutes until softened and thickened.

4 Taste for seasoning, adding more sugar to taste if needed.

5 Can be served immediately, but will keep for 2–3 weeks in a sterilized jar in the refrigerator.

Jackfruit Jalfrezi

Vegans rejoice! This fruity, dairy-free curry is simplicity itself. It's quite hot, but you can tone down the heat by piercing the green chilli rather than slicing it, if you wish. A good jalfrezi should be tongue-tinglingly spicy though, so embrace the heat if you can. *Pictured left with Royal Rice (page 213).*

SERVES 4

3 tbsp vegetable oil

2 brown onions, finely chopped

5cm/2in piece of fresh ginger, peeled and grated

3 garlic cloves, minced

2 x 400g/14oz cans of jackfruit, drained

2 tbsp garam masala

2 tsp ground cumin

1 tsp ground turmeric

¼ tsp chilli powder

1 x 400g/14oz can of chopped tomatoes

2 green bell peppers, deseeded and roughly chopped

1 large green chilli, deseeded and thinly sliced

1 tsp salt

1 tsp sugar

200ml/7fl oz/scant 1 cup water

1 Heat the oil in a large saucepan that has a lid over a medium heat. When hot, add the onions, ginger and garlic, and cook for 7–8 minutes, or until golden brown.

2 Add the drained jackfruit and stir to combine, then cook for 3–4 minutes, or until starting to colour.

3 Add the spices, chopped tomatoes, green bell peppers, green chilli, salt and sugar, along with the measured water. Give everything a good stir together, then turn the heat to low, cover and gently simmer for 15–20 minutes, or until the jackfruit is cooked through and tender.

Bengali Fruit Chaat

So much more than fruit salad, a fruit *chaat* elevates fruit to another dimension with a gently spiced dressing. It might sound counterintuitive, but chaat masala, which is slightly salty and tart, enhances the flavour of any fruit it meets. This tangy salad is very popular in both India and Pakistan and this is my Bengali version. You can play around with the combination of fruits to suit what's in season – I also like to add chopped apple, or some melon when I can get a nice, sweet, ripe one.

SERVES 4

1 orange or 2 clementines, peeled
  and segmented
1 pineapple, peeled and cored,
  flesh cut into small chunks
1 large mango, peeled and flesh
  cut into small chunks
4 kiwi fruit, peeled and sliced
200g/7oz strawberries, sliced
juice of 1 lime
½ tsp chaat masala
½ tsp freshly ground black pepper
¼ tsp black salt (kala namak) (optional)
¼ tsp chilli powder (optional)

1 Combine all the fruit in a large serving bowl, then squeeze over the lime juice and sprinkle over the spices.

2 Mix very gently to combine and serve immediately.

Saffron, Banana & Date Pudding

Is there anything that saffron can't make better? Here, the humble bread and butter pud gets a makeover with a luxurious golden saffron custard. The bread has been swapped out for buttery brioche, the traditional raisins are elevated to sumptuous Medjool dates and I've added a touch of banana for extra sweetness. Definitely not your everyday pud, this is strictly for treat time!

SERVES 8–10

150g/5oz unsalted butter, softened

1 x 400g/14oz brioche loaf, sliced

12 Medjool dates, pitted and quartered

4 bananas, peeled and sliced into
  2cm/¾in rounds

demerara/turbinado sugar, for sprinkling

For the saffron custard

300ml/10½ fl oz/1¼ cups whole milk

200ml/7fl oz/scant 1 cup double/
  heavy cream

a large pinch of saffron strands

100g/3½oz/scant ½ cup golden
  caster/superfine sugar

4 eggs

1 First, make the saffron custard. Place all the custard ingredients in a large bowl and whisk until well combined. Taste and add 1–2 extra tbsp of sugar if needed. Set aside.

2 Butter a large, deep baking dish.

3 Spread both sides of all the brioche slices with butter, then carefully arrange the slices in the baking dish, lining them up so they're standing up slightly. Tuck the chopped dates and banana slices between the brioche slices, dividing them around the dish evenly and scattering some on top, too. Pour over the custard, pressing the brioche slices down into it to ensure it is well absorbed. Set aside for 30 minutes.

4 Meanwhile, preheat the oven to 200°C/400°F/gas mark 6.

5 Cover the baking dish with foil and bake in the oven for 15 minutes.

6 After 15 minutes, remove the foil, sprinkle the top of the pudding with demerara sugar, then place it back into the oven for a further 15 minutes, or until the top is browned and crispy and the filling has puffed up.

7 Let stand for 5–10 minutes before serving.

Lychee & Ginger Granita

This jewel-like granita is so good on its own, but you could also enjoy it with another ice cream (such as vanilla or coconut) for an out-of-the-ordinary dessert. It's easy to make, yet looks special, so is ideal for serving at dinner parties. Handily, it makes exactly the same quantity as most store-bought ice-cream tubs, so you can recycle an old container rather than searching for the ideal Tupperware.

MAKES 1L/35FL OZ

800g/1lb 12oz canned lychees

100g/3½oz/scant ½ cup caster/ superfine sugar

grated zest and juice of 1 lime

100g/3½oz stem ginger (preserved in syrup), very finely chopped

100ml/3½fl oz/scant ½ cup stem ginger syrup (from the jar)

1 Drain the lychees, reserving 200ml/7fl oz/scant 1 cup of the syrup from the cans.

2 Add the drained lychees to a high-speed blender along with the reserved syrup and sugar and blitz until completely smooth.

3 Pour the lychee pulp into a bowl, then add the lime zest and juice, chopped stem ginger and ginger syrup. Give it a good mix, then transfer the mixture to a freezerproof container.

4 Cover and place in the freezer for 1 hour.

5 After 1 hour, remove the container from the freezer and scrape the mixture with a fork to break up the ice crystals.

6 Repeat steps 4 and 5 three times, or until you have a well-crystallized mixture.

7 Your granita is now ready to serve. It will keep in the freezer for 2–3 months, after which time the flavour may diminish.

Vegan Mango Kulfi Loaf

This vegan kulfi is super easy to make and just as delicious as its dairy-based counterpart. Although plant-based creams will never fully whip to the thickness of regular double/heavy cream, you should see it significantly thicken, so make sure to whip for the full time suggested. If you are not planning to eat it all at once, store in the freezer in the loaf pan, wrapped in cling film/plastic wrap to protect it from freezer burn. If you can, seek out Alphonso mango pulp in Asian grocers for a deliciously smooth and rich flavour, or Kesar mango pulp for a milder flavour, although this recipe will work beautifully with any mango purée you can find.

SERVES 4

400ml/ 14fl oz/ 1⅔ cups plant-based double/heavy cream

375g/ 13oz/ 1½ cups canned vegan condensed milk

3–4 green cardamom pods, seeds crushed and husks removed

350ml/ 12fl oz/ 1⅓ cups canned mango purée

To serve

100ml/ 3½fl oz/ scant ½ cup canned mango purée

1 Line a 450g/1lb loaf pan with a double layer of cling film/plastic wrap, leaving some to overhang on all sides.

2 Whip the plant-based cream and vegan condensed milk in a stand mixer or with a hand-held electric whisk, and beat for 8–10 minutes, or until thickened.

3 Fold the crushed cardamom seeds and 200ml/7fl oz/scant 1 cup of the mango purée into the thickened cream mixture. This is your kulfi mixture.

4 Pour a third of the kulfi mixture into the prepared loaf pan. Add 3 tbsp of the remaining mango purée on top and swirl it into the kulfi mixture with a knife.

5 Repeat step 4 until the loaf pan is filled. Cover the surface of the kulfi with the overhanging cling film, then place it in the freezer for 6 hours (or ideally overnight) to set.

6 When ready to serve, place a plate or platter on top of the loaf pan and carefully flip. Remove the cling film and serve cut into slices, drizzled with more mango purée.

Street-Stall Lemonade

This super-refreshing lemonade is hugely popular in India and is commonly found served at streetside stalls or on railway platforms throughout the country. In fact, it is the unusual flavour combination of salt, pepper and spices that make it so uniquely thirst-quenching. There's nothing better on a scorchingly hot or humid day for cooling you down. If serving to kids, you can just add sparkling water and leave out the other additions.

SERVES 1

200g/7oz/scant ½ cup caster/
    superfine sugar
200ml/7fl oz/scant 1 cup water
juice of 3 lemons
juice of 4 limes

To serve

sparkling water, to top up
lemon and lime slices, to decorate
pinch of salt or black salt (kala namak), to taste
pinch of black pepper, to taste
pinch of ground cumin, to taste

1 Add the sugar to a saucepan along with the measured water and bring almost to the boil, stirring regularly to dissolve the sugar. When it is nearly at the boil, turn off the heat and add the lemon and lime juices.

2 Leave to cool completely, then pour the syrup into a sterilized bottle. This can be stored in the refrigerator for 3–4 weeks.

3 To serve, add a couple of tbsp of the syrup to glasses and top up with sparkling water. Add lemon and lime slices, then finish with a sprinkling of salt (or black salt), black pepper and ground cumin, and enjoy.

Chai-Spiced Clementine & Maple Hot Toddy

An Indian take on the classic hot toddy – a gorgeous winter warmer. Swap the clementines for other citrus fruit if you want, such as blood oranges when they are in season. I also think this is a great pick-me-up drink for when you're feeling a bit under the weather.

MAKES 1

1 clementine
1 chai tea bag
3 cloves
1–2 tbsp maple syrup
pinch of black pepper
50ml/1¾fl oz/3 tbsp whisky (optional)

1 Cut a slice out of your clementine to keep for serving, then juice the rest.

2 Use the mug or glass you are going to drink out of to measure some water, then add this to a saucepan along with the chai tea bag, the cloves, maple syrup, clementine juice and a pinch of black pepper. Bring to the boil, then reduce to a low simmer for 5 minutes.

3 Strain the toddy into your mug, then add the whisky (if using) and garnish with the slice of clementine.

7
EGGS & DAIRY

Not vegetables, but a key part of the Indian plant-based kitchen (as long as you aren't vegan) are eggs, cheese, yogurt and milk. This chapter is varied, with enticing breakfasts, classic snacks and some of the richest curries in the book. Of course, milk- and yogurt-based sweets are the jewels of our cuisine, so you will find a few of those treats, too.

Spiced Omelette With Masala Fried Bread

This makes a perfect Indian-style breakfast, or even a light lunch. The omelette itself is substantial and could easily be eaten on its own, but it is even better served with this masala toast and some succulent tomatoes roasted on the vine. Don't forget the ketchup!

SERVES 2

For the roasted tomatoes
250g/9oz cherry tomatoes, on the vine
drizzle of vegetable oil
¼ tsp salt
1 tsp chaat masala

For the spiced omelette
4 eggs
1 small red onion, finely sliced
1 green chilli, finely sliced
50g/2oz Cheddar cheese, finely grated

handful of fresh coriander/cilantro,
    stems and leaves finely chopped
1 tsp salt
1 tsp ground turmeric
1 tbsp vegetable oil
1 tsp cumin seeds

For the masala fried bread
3 tbsp olive oil (or unsalted butter)
1 tsp chaat masala
¼ tsp salt
4 slices of bread

1 Preheat the oven to 220°C/430°F/gas mark 7. Line a baking sheet with baking parchment. Place the cherry tomatoes still on the vine on the baking sheet, drizzle with oil and sprinkle with the salt. Roast in the oven for 10–15 minutes, or until just bursting.

2 Meanwhile, in a small jug, mix together the eggs for the omelette with the onion, chilli, cheese, coriander, salt and turmeric. Add a splash of water and taste for seasoning. Set aside.

3 Start on the masala fried bread. In a bowl, mix together the oil (or butter), chaat masala and salt. Spread about half of the mixture on one side of each slice of bread.

4 Heat a large non-stick frying pan/skillet over a medium heat. When hot, add the bread, oiled/buttered-side down. While the undersides are cooking, spread more oil/butter on the tops. Flip when nicely browned underneath, to cook the other sides. Keep warm.

5 Heat the oil in a non-stick omelette pan over a medium heat. When hot, add the cumin seeds and cook until dark brown. Pour in the egg mixture, cook for 2–3 minutes, or until browning underneath, then flip and cook the omelette on the other side. Divide in half.

6 When the tomatoes are out of the oven, sprinkle with the chaat masala and serve alongside the fried bread and omelettes. My Quick Indian Ketchup (page 83) is great as a sauce here.

Mowgli Sticky Fingers

What happens when the famous Mowgli Sticky Wings (the original recipe for which can be found in *Mowgli Street Food*) go veggie? This is what happens! My classic naughty, sweet, dark glaze works just as beautifully with paneer, so there's no need for anyone to miss out on all the finger-licking fun. These make a great starter or snack and they are good to enjoy with a few other bits of finger food, such as some Broccoli and Coconut Bhajis (page 114), Aloo and Black Gram Chaat (page 32) or Bengali Fruit Chaat (page 155).

SERVES 3-4

2 tbsp date syrup

1 tbsp black treacle/molasses

3 garlic cloves, finely chopped

5cm/2in piece of fresh ginger,
    peeled and finely chopped

1 green chilli, finely chopped

1 tsp garam masala

2 tsp ground cumin

½ tsp black mustard seeds

4 tsp dark rum

juice of 1 lime

2 tbsp white wine vinegar

1 tsp salt

1 x 226g/8oz pack of paneer,
    cut into fingers

2 tbsp vegetable oil

fresh herbs, to garnish (optional)

1 Add all the ingredients, except the paneer, oil and herbs, to a saucepan, stir to combine and set over a medium heat. Bring to the boil, then remove from the heat and allow to cool.

2 Add the paneer fingers to the cooled marinade, mix until well coated and leave for 10 minutes to marinate.

3 Meanwhile, heat the oil in a large non-stick frying pan/skillet over a medium heat. When hot, add the marinated paneer fingers and cook until caramelized all over, drizzling over a little of the marinade if the pan is looking dry.

4 Serve immediately, garnished with fresh herbs, if you want.

Ruby Wraps

The Mowgli Ruby Wrap is always a winner in our restaurants. Soft chapatis are loaded with our delicious tandoori paneer, baby leaf greens and crunchy onions, and generously drizzled with tamarind chutney and a sweet spiced yogurt. You can really go to town on the chutneys if you like – Nisha's Green Chutney (page 83) also brings a fresh spike of flavour to this, as would any of the raitas. Crazy big flavours to blow your mind.

SERVES 2

1 x 226g/8oz pack of paneer, cut into fingers

3 tbsp plain yogurt

1 tbsp tandoori masala

1 tsp salt

¼ tsp ground turmeric

juice of ½ lemon

2 tbsp vegetable oil

2–4 store-bought chapatis (depending on hunger!)

20g/¾oz baby leaf spinach, roughly chopped

½ red onion, finely sliced

100g/3½oz/½ cup fresh pomegranate seeds

For the spiced yogurt

3 tbsp plain yogurt

½ tsp ground cumin

½ tsp ground coriander

juice of ½ lime

¼ tsp salt

½ tsp sugar

Other optional sauces

tamarind chutney (store-bought)

Nisha's Green Chutney (page 83)

Beetroot Raita (page 39)

Spinach Raita (page 139)

1 Place the paneer fingers in a bowl along with the yogurt, tandoori masala, salt, turmeric and lemon juice. Give it a good mix to coat the paneer fingers and set aside for 5 minutes to marinate.

2 Meanwhile, make the spiced yogurt by mixing all the ingredients together in a small bowl. Taste for seasoning and set aside.

3 Heat the oil in a non-stick frying pan/skillet over a medium–high heat. When hot, add the marinated paneer fingers and cook for 3–4 minutes, turning regularly, until golden brown and starting to crisp up all over.

4 Warm your chapatis in the microwave or in a second dry frying pan.

5 To assemble, spread the spiced yoghurt over the chapatis, then load them up with the chopped spinach and onion. Top with the paneer fingers and a sprinkling of pomegranate seeds, and finally drizzle over your chosen sauces and enjoy.

Halloumi Pakora

So simple to make, this gently spiced halloumi is quickly deep-fried and makes a perfect snack. It is lovely dipped into a raita, such as the Spinach Raita (page 139). It can also be served with some chips/fries and my Indian Mushy Peas (page 97) as a veggie alternative to British fish and chips. Make sure you eat them immediately – hot halloumi is heavenly, but turns rather rubbery when cold.

SERVES 2

250g/9oz block of halloumi

½ tsp chilli powder

¼ tsp ground turmeric

1 tsp black pepper

30g/1oz/¼ cup gram flour/besan

½ small bunch of fresh coriander/cilantro, stems and leaves finely chopped

3 tbsp water

1 tsp baking powder

1 tsp chaat masala

1 Drain the halloumi, then cut into thin strips. Place in a mixing bowl along with the chilli powder, turmeric, black pepper, gram flour and coriander, and set aside for 15 minutes.

2 Meanwhile, heat a 4cm/1½in depth of oil in a deep pan to 180°C/350°F. You'll know it's hot enough when you can add a small piece of bread and it sizzles and floats to the surface.

3 Add the measured water and baking powder to the halloumi mixture and give it a good mix. It should form a thick batter and all the halloumi strips should be well coated.

4 When the oil is hot, add the halloumi strips and fry until golden brown and crisp (you might need to do this in batches). Remove with a slotted spoon to drain on paper towels.

5 Sprinkle the halloumi pakora with the chaat masala while still hot and enjoy immediately!

Spiced Cauli Frittata

This gently spiced frittata makes a really substantial lunch and is great served with a simple dressed salad. It's so versatile, the veg can be roasted ahead of time and you can swap in broccoli instead of cauliflower, or sweet potato instead of white potatoes, or swap cheese to dairy-free cheese if needed. You can even use leftover *aloo ghobi* to make it (for a classic *aloo ghobi* – potatoes and cauliflower – try the recipe in my previous book, *Mowgli Street Food*). If flipping it out of the pan scares you, just cut it into slices and put the frying pan straight onto the table to let people help themselves.

SERVES 4–6

1 small cauliflower (500g/1lb 2oz), leaves and florets, chopped into bite-size pieces
1 potato, chopped into small pieces
vegetable oil, for cooking
8 large eggs
60ml/2fl oz/¼ cup milk
80g/3oz Parmesan, finely grated

2 tsp cumin seeds
1 red onion, finely sliced
2 green chillies, sliced
½ tsp ground turmeric
1 tsp ground coriander
½ small bunch of fresh coriander/cilantro, roughly chopped
salt and black pepper, to taste

1 Preheat the oven to 200°C/400°F/gas mark 6.

2 Line a baking sheet with non-stick baking parchment, then add the chopped cauliflower and potatoes with a drizzle of oil and season with salt and pepper. Bake for 30–35 minutes, or until cooked through but still holding their shape, then remove from the oven but leave it on.

3 Meanwhile, add the eggs to a measuring jug along with the milk, Parmesan and a generous pinch of salt and pepper, and whisk until well beaten. Set aside.

4 Heat 2 tbsp of oil in a large, non-stick, ovenproof frying pan/skillet over a medium heat. When hot, add the cumin seeds and let sizzle, then add the sliced onion and green chillies and cook for 4–5 minutes, or until softened.

5 Add the turmeric and ground coriander and cook for a further 1–2 minutes, then add the roasted cauliflower and potatoes, give everything a good mix, then spread it all out in the pan.

6 Evenly pour over the egg mixture, then carefully put the frying pan into the oven and cook for 15 minutes, or until the frittata is puffed up and golden brown.

7 Remove from the oven and let stand for 5–10 minutes before flipping out onto a plate. Garnish with chopped coriander to serve.

Butter Paneer & Peas

This is a new twist on two of our house classics: the Mowgli Paneer and the Mother Butter Chicken (both recipes can be found in my previous book *Mowgli Street Food*), combined to make a meat-free must-have. The paneer is first marinated in a tandoori masala, which imbues it with all those tantalizing flavours. This sweet and comforting curry is rich with butter and will leave you wanting a second helping!

SERVES 4

2 x 226g/8oz blocks of paneer, chopped into large bite-size cubes

2 tbsp tandoori masala

2 tbsp vegetable oil

2 large white onions, thinly sliced

5cm/2in piece of fresh ginger, peeled and finely chopped or grated

4 garlic cloves, finely chopped or grated

2 tsp ground cumin

2 tsp ground coriander

2 tsp garam masala

½ tsp dried fenugreek leaves (kasuri methi)

½ tsp ground turmeric

¼ tsp chilli powder

3 tbsp tomato purée/paste

1 x 400g/14oz can of chopped tomatoes

100g/3½oz/generous ⅓ cup Greek yogurt

250ml/8½fl oz/1 cup water

2 tsp salt

1 tsp sugar

150g/5oz/1 cup frozen garden peas

80g/3oz butter

1 Add the cubed paneer to a bowl along with the tandoori masala and stir until well coated.

2 Heat the oil in a large non-stick pan over a medium heat. When hot, add the sliced onions and cook for 7–8 minutes, or until golden brown. Add the ginger and garlic, and stir for another 4 minutes, then add the spices, tomato purée, chopped tomatoes, Greek yogurt and 150ml/5fl oz/scant ⅔ cup of the water and stir well to combine. Cook for 5 minutes, then remove from the heat and let cool slightly.

3 When the mixture is cooled, blitz with a hand-held blender until smooth.

4 Return the blended sauce to the pan, add the remaining 100ml/3½fl oz/scant ½ cup water and bring to the boil, then add the marinated paneer, salt and sugar, reduce to a simmer and cook for 5–6 minutes, or until the paneer has softened.

5 Stir in the peas and butter, and cook for a final 2 minutes before serving.

Two-Ingredient Naan

I call this two-ingredient naan because the only crucial ingredients are flour and yogurt, and at a push you can make perfectly good breads with just those elements. I urge you to include the tasty extras though, for delicious, freshly made breads that are excellent for carrying curry.

SERVES 6

250g/9oz/2 cups self-raising flour,
    plus extra for dusting

1 tsp salt

2 tsp nigella seeds

2 tsp cumin seeds

200g/7oz/generous ¾ cup Greek yogurt

50g/2oz ghee or butter, melted, for brushing

1 Combine the flour in a large bowl with the salt, nigella seeds and cumin seeds. Make a well in the middle, then add the yogurt, stirring with a wooden spoon at first to combine, then using your hands to bring it together into a dough.

2 Tip the dough onto a lightly floured work surface, then knead by hand for 4–5 minutes, or until smooth. Divide into 6 equal pieces and roll each one out into a thin oval shape.

3 Heat a non-stick frying pan/skillet over a high heat. When smoking hot, add your first naan and let it cook for 2–3 minutes, or until bubbles form on the surface, then flip and cook the other side in the same way.

4 Transfer the cooked naan to a large piece of foil, brush the top with ghee or butter then enclose in the foil to keep it warm. Continue with the remaining naan, adding each cooked one to the foil parcel to keep warm before serving.

Egg, Ginger & Spinach Curry

This is a staple fare. A good egg curry is in the repertoire of many Indian families – it's one of those dishes that seems to evoke nostalgia in everyone. This is a lovely, substantial dish with a good kick of ginger and heat from the green chillies, which can of course be adjusted to suit your own taste and heat tolerance level.

SERVES 4

8 large eggs

4–6 tbsp vegetable oil

2 tsp cumin seeds

2 tsp black mustard seeds

2 brown onions, finely chopped

7.5cm/3in piece of fresh ginger, peeled
    and finely chopped or grated

4 garlic cloves, peeled and finely chopped
    or grated

½ tsp ground turmeric

½ tsp chilli powder

2 tsp ground cumin

1½ tsp salt

1 tsp sugar

1 x 400g/14oz can of chopped tomatoes

200ml/7fl oz/scant 1 cup water

200g/7oz baby spinach

1 tbsp garam masala

2 green chillies, finely sliced

1 Hard-boil the eggs, then cool and peel. Cut the eggs in half, then set aside.

2 Heat 4 tbsp of the oil in a wide-based pan over a medium heat. When hot, add the cumin and mustard seeds and cook until dark brown. Add the onions and cook for 5–6 minutes, or until starting to soften, then add the ginger and garlic. Fry for 1–2 minutes, then add the spices, salt and sugar.

3 Add the chopped tomatoes with the measured water and the baby spinach, bring to a simmer, then stir until the spinach starts to wilt.

4 Heat the remaining 2 tbsp of oil in a separate pan. When hot, add the halved eggs and fry until they become gnarled, cracked and brown all over.

5 Add the eggs and garam masala to the sauce and cook for a final 3–4 minutes, or until heated through.

5 Serve garnished with the sliced green chillies.

Egg & Cauliflower Curry

This is a new spin on the classic egg curry that I would often have while growing up. The spiced, slightly crispy eggs with a little bite to them are utterly delicious. Mashed into rice or eaten with bread, there is a substantialness to them that is almost meaty. The addition of the cauliflower florets serves to further bulk up this saucy curry, making it a satisfying, filling supper for two. It is easily doubled to feed more.

SERVES 2

3 tbsp vegetable oil

1 tbsp panch phoron

1 large red onion, finely sliced

5cm/2in piece of fresh ginger, peeled and finely chopped

4 garlic cloves, finely chopped

1 green chilli, finely chopped

1 tsp ground turmeric

¼ tsp chilli powder

200g/7oz chopped tomatoes

150g/5oz cauliflower, broken into small florets

1 tsp salt

½ tsp sugar

200ml/7fl oz/scant 1 cup water, or more as needed

small bunch of fresh coriander/cilantro, finely chopped, leaves and stalks kept separate

1 tsp garam masala

1 tsp English mustard paste mixed with 1 tbsp water

juice of ½ lemon

For the eggs

1 tbsp vegetable oil

4 eggs, hard-boiled and peeled

½ tsp ground turmeric

½ tsp salt

1 Heat the oil in a medium non-stick saucepan that has a lid over a medium heat. When hot, add the panch phoron and let sizzle briefly (be careful not to burn the fenugreek seeds), then add the onion. Cook for 5–6 minutes, or until starting to soften.

2 Add the ginger, garlic and green chilli and cook for 2–3 minutes, or until fragrant. Stir in the turmeric, chilli powder and chopped tomatoes, then stir in the cauliflower florets. Add the salt, sugar and measured water, cover and simmer for 5–6 minutes until the cauliflower is cooked through.

3 Meanwhile, prepare the eggs. Heat the oil in a non-stick frying pan/skillet over a medium heat. Add the hard-boiled eggs, turmeric and salt and stir until the eggs have gnarled, cracked and browned all over, then remove from the heat.

4 When the cauliflower is cooked, gently stir in the hard-boiled eggs, chopped coriander stalks, garam masala and mustard mixture. Squeeze in the lemon juice, taste for seasoning and add a splash more water if needed. Serve garnished with the chopped coriander leaves.

Paneer Kofta & Potato Curry

Koftas don't have to be meat-based – in India, vegetarian koftas are also common, made from paneer or potato and sometimes gourd or other mixed veg. I love paneer koftas. These golden cheesy fried dumplings soak up all the delicious flavours of the masala here for a divine, richly comforting curry. It is very slightly more time-consuming than my usual dishes, but it is so worth the extra effort. The recipe is easily doubled to serve four.

SERVES 2

For the kofta

226g/8oz paneer

2 tbsp cornflour/cornstarch

¼ tsp ground turmeric

¼ tsp chilli powder

½ tsp salt

2 tbsp water

6 tbsp vegetable oil, for cooking

For the curry

3 tbsp vegetable oil

2 bay leaves

1 tsp cumin seeds

1 green chilli, finely chopped

5cm/2in piece of fresh ginger, peeled and finely chopped

200g/7oz chopped tomatoes

1 tsp salt

1 tsp sugar

2 tsp ground cumin

½ tsp ground turmeric

1 tsp ground coriander

150g/5oz white potato, peeled and chopped into 2.5cm/1in chunks

200ml/7fl oz/scant 1 cup water

1 tsp garam masala

juice of ½ lemon

1 small bunch of coriander/cilantro, leaves and stems finely chopped

1 To make the kofta, grate the paneer onto a large plate, then add the remaining kofta ingredients, except the oil, and mix together with your hands, squeezing until well combined. Divide into 12 equal-size balls.

2 For the curry, heat the oil in a saucepan that has a lid over a medium heat. When hot, add the bay leaves and cumin seeds and fry until the seeds are dark brown, then add the green chilli and ginger. Cook for 2–3 minutes, or until fragrant, then stir in the chopped tomatoes, salt, sugar and ground spices (except the garam masala). Add the potatoes and measured water, cover and cook for 15–20 minutes, or until the potatoes are cooked through.

3 Meanwhile, heat the oil for cooking the kofta in a large non-stick frying pan/skillet over a medium-high heat. When hot, add the paneer kofta and cook for 4–5 minutes, turning them until browned all over.

4 Add the paneer kofta to the curry (with a splash more water if it seems a bit dry), stir in the garam masala and lemon juice, then garnish with the coriander and enjoy.

Kolkata Chilli Paneer

This is a dish very particular to the city of Kolkata, where Hakka Chinese immigrants developed a style of cooking that really took off in 18th-century Bengal, fusing elements of their home cuisine with traditional Indian flavours. You will find this Indo-Chinese style of food served in the city's restaurants and street food outlets, but it has become so popular that many Indian households have adopted it into their repertoires. Sweet and sour, hot and sticky, it's quite addictively good. This is easily doubled to serve four.

SERVES 2

226g/8oz block of paneer, cut into
    bite-size cubes
30g/1oz/¼ cup cornflour/cornstarch
20g/¾oz/scant ¼ cup plain/
    all-purpose flour
1 tbsp soy sauce
1 tbsp water
4 tbsp vegetable oil
4 spring onions/scallions, finely sliced,
    greens and whites kept separate
2.5cm/1in piece of fresh ginger, finely
    chopped into matchsticks

4 garlic cloves, finely sliced
2–3 green chillies, finely sliced
1 red bell pepper, deseeded and
    chopped into small chunks

For the sauce

2 tbsp soy sauce
1 tbsp rice vinegar
2 tbsp tomato ketchup
2 tbsp chilli sauce (such as sriracha)
1 tbsp honey
2 tbsp water

1 Add the paneer cubes to a bowl with the cornflour, flour, soy sauce and water. Stir until well coated.

2 Stir all the sauce ingredients together in a bowl and set aside.

3 Heat 2 tbsp of the oil in a wide pan over a medium heat. When hot, add the paneer cubes and fry on all sides until golden brown. Remove to a plate lined with paper towels.

4 Heat the remaining oil in the same pan. When hot, add the spring onion whites, sliced ginger, garlic and green chillies. Cook for 3–4 minutes, then add the bell pepper. Cook for 4–5 minutes, or until softening, then add the paneer back to the pan and cook for a further 3–4 minutes, or until softened.

5 Add the sauce to the pan and bring to a simmer, stirring until everything is coated. Garnish with the spring onion greens and serve immediately.

Grandmother's Rice Pudding

Making rice pudding was the way my mother showed her love for her grandchildren. As ageing hands become arthritic, this is one of the kindly stirrings a grandma can still do to demonstrate warmth and care for her family. Known as *kheer*, this fragrant, sweet pudding is one of India's most popular desserts and it's likely that the dish originated there due to our ancient rice-growing culture. Not dissimilar to the classic British rice pudding, its subtle cardamom spicing lifts it out of the realm of school dinner doldrums to another level of deliciousness. This simple, creamy home comfort can be enjoyed hot or cold. The pudding and topping can be made separately ahead of time, but if you do this, remember to add some extra milk to the pudding to loosen it up when reheating, as it will thicken as it cools. Swap out the apples for other fruit, if you want, or the almonds for other nuts.

SERVES 4

1l/35fl oz/4¼ cups whole milk, or as needed

1 large cinnamon stick

2 green cardamom pods, crushed in a pestle and mortar

2 Indian bay leaves (tej patta)

500g/1lb 2oz/2½ cups pudding rice

80g/3oz/⅓ cup golden caster/superfine sugar, or as needed

To serve

15g/½oz unsalted butter

1 Granny Smith apple, diced

100ml/3½fl oz/scant ½ cup date syrup

30g/1oz/⅓ cup flaked/slivered almonds, toasted

1 Combine the milk, cinnamon stick, cardamom pods (seeds and husks) and bay leaves in a medium non-stick saucepan and bring almost to the boil over a medium heat. Keep at a fast simmer for 10–15 minutes, or until reduced by a third, stirring continuously.

2 Once the milk has reduced, add the pudding rice and sugar and reduce to a low simmer. Cook for 30–40 minutes, stirring occasionally, until the rice is cooked. If you find it is thickening too much but the rice isn't quite cooked yet, add a splash more milk.

3 Meanwhile, heat the butter in a small frying pan/skillet over a medium heat. Add the apple and fry until golden.

4 Taste the rice and add more sugar if needed. If you like, you can fish out the cardamom husks and the cinnamon stick at this point (or leave them in and warn others when serving that they might find whole spices on eating). Serve with the pan-fried apples, drizzled with the date syrup and sprinkled with the toasted flaked almonds.

Baked Rose Yogurt

This is a typical Bengali dessert. Baked yogurt is gently sweetened with a light tang and has a firm texture rather like cheesecake. For a pretty pink colour, try to find a genuine Indian rose syrup (in the Asian aisles of supermarkets or in Indian grocers). Other rose syrups will not give such a depth of colour, but will still taste wonderful. You can either make this in a large dish or in individual dishes. Either way, it is the perfect dessert for entertaining as it can be made ahead of time and is super easy.

SERVES 4

250g/9oz/1 cup full-fat Greek yogurt
125g/4oz/generous ⅓ cup condensed milk
3 tbsp rose syrup

1 tsp vanilla extract
1 tbsp finely chopped pistachios
1 tbsp dried rose petals

1 Preheat the oven to 180°C/350°F/gas mark 4. Bring a kettle of water to the boil.

2 In a jug, mix together the Greek yogurt and condensed milk until well combined without any lumps, then add the rose syrup and vanilla extract.

3 Place 4 ovenproof ramekins in a baking dish, then carefully divide the yogurt mixture among them. Pour enough boiling water into the baking dish to come halfway up the sides of the ramekins, then cover the dish tightly with kitchen foil.

4 Bake in the oven for 20–25 minutes, or until set, then remove from the oven and let cool.

5 When cool, place in the fridge and leave to set for at least 2 hours, or ideally overnight.

6 Serve decorated with the chopped pistachios and dried rose petals.

8

MUSHROOMS & MORE!

Nutritious mushrooms make for substantial and satisfying additions to many Indian meals and are a must in the plant-based kitchen. In this chapter, you will also find a few recipes that defied categorization, such as ones for plant-based proteins (very useful for meat-free curries that mimic meaty ones, if that's your thing), a sweetcorn ribs recipe, some rice-based accompaniments and a few dishes featuring nuts, including a cheeky non-dairy Coconut Panna Cotta (page 215).

Tandoori Tofu Kebabs
with Mango & Lime Glaze

Great as a party nibble or starter, these gently spiced tandoori kebabs have a toothsome sticky mango and lime marinade that is incredibly moreish. They make an ideal meat-free offering at a summer barbecue and can be barbecued just as easily as they are grilled or broiled. And the recipe is easily doubled or tripled to serve more.

SERVES 2–3

400g/14oz firm tofu

2 tbsp tandoori spice mix (store-bought)

3 tbsp plain yogurt (or dairy free yogurt alternative)

1 tbsp vegetable oil, plus extra for drizzling

handful of fresh coriander/cilantro, chopped

½ lime, cut into wedges

salt and black pepper, to taste

For the glaze

3 tbsp mango chutney

1 tbsp sriracha sauce

juice of ½ lime

1 If using wooden skewers, soak about 5 skewers in water for 30 minutes.

2 Preheat a grill/broiler to high and line a baking sheet with kitchen foil.

3 Drain the tofu block and dry thoroughly, then cut into 20 equal-size cubes. Place them in a bowl with the tandoori spice mix, yogurt and oil. Season generously with salt and pepper (I use about 2 tsp of salt) and gently mix together until the cubes are coated. Set aside to marinate for 10 minutes.

4 Meanwhile, mix together the glaze ingredients in a bowl.

5 Thread the marinated tofu onto skewers. Drizzle the baking sheet with plenty of oil, then arrange the skewers on the sheet. Grill/broil for 8 minutes, turning after 4 minutes.

6 Remove from the grill, then brush the mango and lime glaze over all the skewers. Pop back under the grill for 2 minutes, or until charred and sticky.

7 Serve the skewers on a platter, garnished with the chopped coriander and lime wedges.

Enoki Mushroom Fritters

Crispy and light, I find these little mushroom bhajis irresistible. It's very hard to stop popping them into your mouth once you start. A lovely starter for a sharing feast – don't forget the chutneys or raitas to serve alongside.

SERVES 4 AS A STARTER

2 tbsp rice flour

100g/3½oz/scant 1 cup gram flour/besan

1 tbsp cumin seeds

large handful of fresh coriander/cilantro, chopped

2 garlic cloves, finely chopped

2 tsp salt

¼ tsp chilli powder

¼ tsp bicarbonate of soda/baking soda

100–150ml/3½–5fl oz/scant ½–⅔ cup water

vegetable oil, for deep-frying

150g/5oz enoki mushrooms

1 Combine the rice flour, gram flour, cumin seeds, chopped coriander, garlic, salt, chilli powder and bicarbonate of soda in a large mixing bowl. Slowly pour in the measured water, mixing as you go, until you have a thick batter the consistency of double/heavy cream (you may not need all the water).

2 Meanwhile, heat a 2.5cm/1in depth of oil in a deep-fat fryer or heavy-based saucepan to 180°C/350°F. You'll know it's hot enough when you can add a small piece of bread and it sizzles and floats to the surface.

3 When the oil is hot, dip the enoki mushrooms into the batter and fry in batches until golden brown and crisp. Remove with a slotted spoon to a plate lined with paper towels t o absorb excess oil.

4 Serve immediately and enjoy with your favourite chutneys or raitas.

Spiced Scrambled Tofu Wraps

Great for a vegan breakfast, scrambled tofu is not dissimilar to scrambled eggs. Given a punchy spicing, and rolled into tortilla wraps (or chapatis work just as well), it will certainly wake you up in the morning!

SERVES 2

2 tbsp vegetable oil

1 x 280g/10oz block of firm tofu, well drained

1 tsp salt

1 green chilli, finely sliced

4 spring onions/scallions, finely sliced

½ tsp ground turmeric

1 tsp ground coriander

1 tsp ground cumin

a pinch of coarse chaat masala

4 small soft tortilla wraps (store-bought)

1 tomato, roughly chopped

handful of fresh coriander/cilantro, leaves and stems roughly chopped

a squeeze of lemon juice

1 Heat 1 tbsp of the oil in a non-stick frying pan/skillet over a high heat. When hot, crumble in the tofu (in small pieces) and add the salt. Leave to cook for 3–4 minutes without moving it, then stir and cook for a further 3–4 minutes, or until starting to crisp up all over. Remove to a plate and set aside.

2 Return the pan to a medium heat with the remaining 1 tbsp of oil. When hot, add the green chilli and spring onions, cook for 2–3 minutes, or until softened, then add the tofu back to the pan.

3 Add the spices and stir to combine. Cook for 2 minutes, or until fragrant, then remove from the heat.

4 Meanwhile, warm the tortillas according to the packet instructions.

5 Fill the tortillas with the scrambled tofu and top with the chopped tomato and coriander. Add a squeeze of lemon juice. Put your favourite chutneys on the table to serve alongside and dig in!

Lip-Smacking Corn Ribs
with Green Chilli Mayo

You've probably seen these if you've been eating out recently – corn ribs are the new trendy alternative to pork or beef ribs. My spicy version is completely mouth-watering and so fun to eat. The tangy chaat masala sprinkle and the acidity from the lime juice squeezed on at the end are essential to lift these from ordinary to out of this world, so don't miss them out! Cooking for kids? Just leave out the chilli and serve with a simple lime mayo.

SERVES 4 AS A STARTER

2 corn cobs

¼ tsp ground turmeric

½ tsp chilli powder

2 tsp ground cumin

2 tsp smoked paprika

2 tbsp vegetable oil

salt and black pepper, to taste

For the green chilli mayo

100ml/3½fl oz/scant ½ cup mayonnaise

1 garlic clove, finely chopped or grated

1–2 green chillies, finely chopped

juice of ½ lime

To garnish

1 tsp chaat masala

sliced spring onions/scallions (optional)

sliced red chillies (optional)

sprinkle of sesame seeds (optional)

1 large lime, chopped into wedges

1 Using a heavy, sharp knife, cut the corn cobs into quarters lengthways. This is hard work, but essential for getting a good curl to the corn ribs. Take your time and use a rocking, seesaw motion to get through the cobs. Place in a bowl along with the spices and oil, season with salt and pepper and mix well. Set aside to marinate for 15–20 minutes.

2 Meanwhile, preheat the oven to 200°C/400°F/gas mark 6 and line a baking sheet with non-stick baking parchment. Arrange the marinated corn ribs on the baking sheet and bake in the oven for 20–25 minutes, or until curled and crispy.

3 In a bowl, mix together the ingredients for the green chilli mayo. Taste and check you are happy with the balance of flavours.

4 Arrange the crispy corn ribs on a platter and sprinkle with the chaat masala and the sliced spring onions, chillies and sesame seeds, if using. Serve with the lime wedges on the side and the green chilli mayo for dipping.

Mowgli Soya Keema Pau

This is a twist on my Mowgli Lamb Keema (the original recipe of which can be found in *Mowgli Street Food*), swapping in veggie mince and serving it as the classic Indian street food known as *keema pav*. It is the Indian equivalent of a burger, with spicy mince and peas served in a bun piled with some tangy salad. It is brilliant for when you have friends over – kids in particular love it (you can adjust the chilli level). You can make the keema ahead of time, but add a splash of water when reheating.

SERVES 4

2 tbsp vegetable oil

1 brown onion, peeled and finely diced

2.5cm/1in piece of fresh ginger, peeled

3 garlic cloves, peeled

2–3 green chillies, stalks removed

2 tbsp tomato purée/paste

¼ tsp ground turmeric

2 tsp ground cumin

1 tsp ground coriander

2 tsp garam masala

2 tomatoes, finely chopped

2 tsp sugar

300ml/10½fl oz/1¼ cups boiling water

300g/10½oz frozen soya mince/
    meatless grounds

80g/3oz/½ cup frozen peas

4 burger buns

salt, to taste

½ small bunch coriander/cilantro,
    roughly chopped, to serve

1 Heat the oil in a wide pan that has a lid over a medium heat. When hot, add most of the onion (keep back a handful to serve) along with a generous pinch of salt and cook for 5–6 minutes, or until softened.

2 Meanwhile, blitz the ginger, garlic and green chillies to a paste in a food processor.

3 When the onions are soft, add the ginger/garlic/chilli paste along with the tomato purée and ground spices, and stir to combine. Add the chopped tomato (reserving some to serve), sugar and 2 tsp salt and cook for 3–4 minutes until the tomatoes start to break down.

4 Pour in the boiling water and bring to a simmer, then add the soya mince and peas. Pop the lid on the pan and cook for a final 3–4 minutes.

5 Meanwhile, toast your burger buns.

6 Fill the toasted buns with the veggie keema and garnish with the reserved tomatoes and onions. Sprinkle over the chopped coriander and enjoy. Alternatively, put everything on the table in bowls and let people build their own.

Monsoon Mushroom Madras

Mushrooms only flourish in India during the damp monsoon season, so this is very much a seasonal dish for my family. This dairy-free, slightly fiery curry is ideal for mushroom lovers – and will work with whatever type of mushroom you have to hand – I like a combination of chestnut/cremini and wild or shiitake. The dish is very flexible and can be made drier or with more of a gravy by adjusting the quantity of liquid during cooking. Serve with rice or flatbreads for scooping.

SERVES 4

2.5cm/1in piece of fresh ginger, peeled and roughly chopped

2 garlic cloves, peeled

2–3 green chillies, stalks removed

2 tbsp vegetable oil

2 tsp cumin seeds

2 banana shallots, peeled and finely sliced

2 tbsp tomato purée/paste

1 tsp ground cumin

1 tsp ground coriander

½ tsp ground turmeric

500g/1lb 2oz mixed mushrooms, sliced

100ml/3½fl oz/scant ½ cup water

1 tsp garam masala

1 tsp amchur/mango powder

juice of ½ lemon

salt, to taste

large handful of fresh coriander/cilantro, chopped

1 Add the ginger, garlic and green chillies to a food processor and blitz to a paste.

2 Heat the oil in a large wide-based pan over a medium heat. When hot, add the cumin seeds and let them sizzle until they turn a dark brown colour, then add the shallots with a generous pinch of salt. Cook for 4–5 minutes, or until softened, then add the ginger, garlic and chilli paste, and cook for 1 minute, then stir in the tomato purée and ground spices.

3 Add the mushrooms to the pan and stir to coat in the spices. Pour in the measured water, then simmer for 8–10 minutes, or until the mushrooms are cooked through and the sauce has thickened slightly. Add a splash more water if it's looking dry at any point.

4 Finish with the garam masala, amchur, lemon juice and 2 tsp salt. Taste for seasoning, then serve garnished with the chopped coriander.

Golden Peanut Pilau

I've taken inspiration from South Indian food for this easy-to-make, vegan pilau.
The hint of crunch from the peanuts and the gentle golden hue lent by the turmeric
makes it feel a little bit special. It goes well with any curry and is even nice on its own
as a snack. If you're not entirely plant-based, you can swap the vegetable oil to ghee
for an even more indulgent flavour, or you could swap the peanuts for cashews if you
are feeling very extravagant.

SERVES 2

1 tbsp vegetable oil (or ghee)

1 stalk of curry leaves, leaves (about 10)
    stripped from stalk

1 tsp ground turmeric

50g/2oz/⅓ cup unsalted peanuts,
    roughly chopped

juice of ½ lemon

150g/5oz/¾ cup basmati rice, washed
    and drained

2 tsp salt, or to taste

300ml/10½fl oz/1¼ cups water

1 Heat a medium saucepan over a medium-low heat. When hot, add the oil (or ghee) and
the curry leaves. Once they're sizzling, add the turmeric, chopped peanuts and lemon juice
and stir to combine.

2 Add the drained rice along with the salt, then
cover with the measured water and bring to the
boil. Once boiling, reduce to a simmer, cover and
cook for 10–12 minutes, or until all the water has
been absorbed. Remove from the heat and set
aside with the lid on for 5 minutes – this allows
the rice to steam.

3 Fluff up the rice with a fork and serve with
your favourite curry!

Mushroom Tikka Masala

Tikka masala might not be an authentic Indian dish, but there's no denying its popularity. It's easy to make it meat-free. Pick your mushrooms of choice and let them simmer in this rich, sweet, spiced tomato and yogurt sauce. Serve with rice or breads, although I like breads to soak up all that thick sauce.

SERVES 2

4 tbsp vegetable oil

1 large white onion, thinly sliced

2.5cm/1in piece of fresh ginger, peeled and finely chopped or grated

2 garlic cloves, finely chopped or grated

2 tsp ground cumin

1 tsp ground coriander

¼ tsp ground cardamom

¼ tsp ground cinnamon

¼ tsp ground fenugreek

½ tsp ground turmeric

¼ tsp chilli powder

1 tbsp tandoori masala

1 tbsp tomato purée/paste

1 x 200g/7oz can of chopped tomatoes

3 tbsp Greek yogurt

1½ tsp salt

1 tsp sugar

100ml/3½fl oz/scant ½ cup water, plus 3 tbsp

250g/9oz mixed mushrooms, chopped or torn into large bite-size pieces

1 Heat 2 tbsp of the oil in a large non-stick saucepan that has a lid over a medium heat. When hot, add the onion and cook for 7–8 minutes, or until golden brown.

2 Add the ginger and garlic, and stir for another minute, then add the spices, tomato purée, chopped tomatoes, Greek yogurt, salt and sugar. Add the 3 tbsp of water and stir well to combine. Cook for 5 minutes, then remove from the heat and let cool slightly.

3 When cooled, blitz with a hand-held blender until smooth.

4 Meanwhile, wipe out the pan with paper towels and return to a medium-high heat with the remaining 2 tbsp vegetable oil. When hot, add the mushrooms and cook for 4–5 minutes, or until coloured all over.

5 Return the blended sauce to the pan along with the 100ml/3½fl oz/scant ½ cup water and bring to the boil, then cover and reduce to a simmer. Cook for 5 minutes, or until the mushrooms are cooked through. You may need to add a splash more water if it's looking a little dry.

Bengali Plain Flour Puris

This is my workaday recipe for puris given a slight twist. Puris are traditionally made at home with wholemeal/whole wheat flour (chapati atta), but some restaurants and street food vendors use plain/all-purpose flour (maida). They are just as tasty, and seem to absorb a little less oil when frying. Crisp, soft and fluffy, these breads are a delicious accompaniment to any of the curries in this book.

MAKES 14

250g/9oz/2 cups plain/all-purpose flour,
    plus extra for dusting
1 tbsp vegetable oil or ghee

1 tsp salt
100ml/3½fl oz/scant ½ cup water
vegetable oil, for deep-frying

1 Combine the flour in a large bowl with the oil (or ghee, if using) and salt. Slowly pour in 80ml/3fl oz/5 tbsp of the water, stirring as you go with a wooden spoon or your hand to bring the dough together. If you need more water, add it splash by splash until you have a dough that holds together. Knead for 5–6 minutes, or until smooth and medium-firm, then cover with a dish towel and leave to rest for 15 minutes.

2 When the dough has rested, divide it into 14 balls of equal size. On a lightly floured work surface and with a floured rolling pin, roll out each ball of dough to a thin circle (6–8cm/2¼–3¼in in diameter).

3 Heat a 5–7.5cm/2–3in depth of oil in a deep-fat fryer or heavy-based saucepan to 180°C/350°F. You'll know it's hot enough when you can add a tiny ball of dough and it sizzles and floats to the surface.

4 When the oil is ready, slowly slide in a puri and fry for 2 minutes on each side, or until starting to brown. Remove with a slotted spoon to drain on paper towels. Repeat with the remaining puris and serve with your curries of choice!

Oyster Mushroom Bhuna

This is my classic bhuna recipe, which works pefectly with mushrooms swapped in for what would normally be the meat component. I like to use an oyster mushroom here, as it brings that slightly meaty texture that a good bhuna needs. And I add a bit of extra bulk with half a can of chickpeas/garbanzo beans. It's a rich dish that can take a bit of Nisha's Green Chutney (page 83) on the side and Bengali Puris (page 209) for absorbing that flavourful sauce.

SERVES 4–6

5 tbsp vegetable oil

1 large white onion, cut in half and thinly sliced

7.5cm/3in piece of fresh root ginger, peeled and grated

4 garlic cloves, minced

800g/1lb 12oz oyster mushrooms, cleaned and any large ones torn into smaller chunks

½ tsp ground turmeric

½ tsp chilli powder

2 tbsp garam masala

1 tbsp ground cumin

200g/7oz canned chickpeas/garbanzo beans, drained and rinsed

2 heaped tbsp canned chopped tomatoes

150ml/5fl oz/⅔ cup water

2 tsp salt

1 green chilli, pierced

small bunch of fresh coriander/cilantro, leaves and stalks chopped

Bengali Puris (page 209) and Nisha's Green Chutney (page 83), to serve

1 Heat the oil in a large, heavy-based pan over a medium heat. When hot, add the onion, ginger and garlic, and fry for 8 minutes, or until the onion has softened and turned golden brown.

2 Add the mushrooms, increase the heat to high and cook until golden brown, then add the turmeric, chilli powder, garam masala and ground cumin and stir to coat the mushrooms with the spices.

3 Add the chickpeas and chopped tomatoes, followed by the measured water, salt and pierced chilli and bring to the boil, then reduce the heat to low and simmer gently, partially covered, for about 15 minutes, adding a splash more water if the pan is looking a little dry.

4 Finish by stirring through the fresh coriander and serve with puris and chutney.

Numbing Pepper Rice

Szechuan-style cooking is famous in India. Also known as Indo-Chinese cuisine, it is very popular, particularly in Kolkata, where it began with the combining of both cuisines after Chinese migration to the city. Sichuan peppercorns will give this fried rice dish an authentic flavour and that classic numbing/tingly effect on your palate, but you can leave them out if you can't find them. This makes a perfect supper or lunch dish on its own.

SERVES 4

2.5cm/1in piece of fresh ginger, peeled

3 garlic cloves, peeled

1 red chilli, stalk removed

2 tbsp vegetable oil

1 tsp Sichuan peppercorns, crushed
to a powder (optional)

1 red bell pepper, deseeded and
roughly chopped

3 spring onions/scallions, finely sliced,
greens and whites kept separate

100g/3½oz baby corn, roughly chopped

100g/3½oz green beans, finely chopped

1 carrot, peeled and finely chopped

1kg/2lb 4oz pre-cooked basmati rice
(those store-bought pouches are ideal)

salt, to taste

For the sauce

1 tbsp white wine vinegar

5 tbsp tomato ketchup

2 tbsp soy sauce

2 tbsp chilli sauce

½ tsp sugar

1 Add the ginger, garlic and chilli to a food processor and blitz until finely chopped.

2 Combine the sauce ingredients in a bowl along with 2 tbsp water and mix until combined.

3 Heat the oil a large wide-based pan that has a lid over a medium heat. When hot, add the ginger/garlic/chilli paste along with the crushed Sichuan pepper and cook for 2–3 minutes, or until fragrant.

4 Add all the chopped veg (except the spring onion greens) to the pan along with a splash of water and season with salt. Cover with the pan lid and cook for 8–10 minutes, or until the veg is softened but still with a little bite.

5 Add the rice and use a wooden spoon to break up any large clumps, then add the sauce and stir to combine. Add a splash more water if the pan looks dry!

6 Serve the rice garnished with the reserved spring onion greens.

Royal Rice

Delicately fragrant with spices and rich with fruit and nuts, this rice dish is traditionally served on special occasions. Known as *mishti pulao* (sweet rice), I call this Bengali speciality "royal" as it feels extravagant and I serve it as a treat on festival days and at family feasts. With a light undertone of sweetness and a heavenly golden colour, it will perfectly accompany any of the curries in this book. *Pictured on page 153.*

SERVES 4–6

2 tbsp ghee

2.5cm/1in cinnamon stick

3 green cardamom pods

2 cloves

2 Indian bay leaves

50g/2oz/⅓ cup cashews

50g/2oz/scant 1½ cups raisins

1 tsp ground turmeric

1 tsp ground cumin

a large pinch of saffron strands (about ½ tsp)

250g/9oz/1¼ cups basmati rice, well rinsed and drained

1½ tsp salt

1 tsp sugar

500ml/17fl oz/2 cups water

1 Heat the ghee in a large saucepan that has a lid over a medium heat. Once melted, add the whole spices and bay leaves, and sizzle for 1 minute before stirring in the cashews and raisins. Add the ground spices, saffron, rice, salt and sugar, and stir until well coated, then add the measured water. Bring to the boil, then cover and reduce to a simmer. Cook for 10–12 minutes, or until all the water is absorbed and the rice is cooked.

2 Turn off the heat, but leave the lid on the pan for 5 minutes so the rice can steam to pillowy softness before serving.

Coconut Panna Cotta

This is my vegan take on panna cotta. It's quite fresh and light and great for people who don't have a sweet tooth – I don't and I often find Indian desserts a bit cloying as a result. Made with creamy coconut milk, it doesn't set as firm as a regular panna cotta – it's a little softer – but that's okay. I like to make it in individual bowls or small glasses rather than worry about turning it out of a larger vessel, which makes it ideal for dinner parties. You can also make it ahead of time and keep it in the refrigerator until you're ready to serve, adding the passionfruit and coconut topping at the last minute.

SERVES 4
400ml/14fl oz canned coconut milk
1 tsp vanilla extract
200ml/7fl oz/scant 1 cup maple syrup
100ml/3½fl oz/scant ½ cup water
6.5g/¼oz sachet of vege-gel (vegetarian gelling powder)
grated zest of 2 limes and juice of 1 lime

To decorate
pulp of 2 passionfruit
1 tbsp desiccated/dried shredded coconut, toasted

1 Combine the coconut milk, vanilla, maple syrup and measured water in a saucepan and stir to combine. Sprinkle over the vege-gel and mix to dissolve, then add the lime zest and juice.

2 Set the pan over a low heat and gently bring to the boil, then remove from the heat.

3 Divide the mixture equally among 4 small heatproof bowls. Put into the refrigerator for at least 4–6 hours, or ideally overnight, to set.

4 To serve, remove from the fridge and top with the passionfruit pulp, sprinkle with the toasted coconut and enjoy.

Chocolate & Cardamon Shortbread Cookies

These crumbly little shortbread cookies are fragrant with cardamom and vanilla and the sharp drizzle of dark chocolate just makes them feel luxurious. A treat for chai-time (or any time!).

MAKES 12

100g/3½oz/generous ¾ cup plain/ all-purpose flour

50g/2oz/½ cup gram flour/besan

2 tbsp semolina

½ tsp baking powder

1 tsp vanilla bean paste

seeds from 3 green cardamom pods

100g/3½oz/generous ¾ cup icing/ confectioners' sugar

100g/3½oz unsalted butter, melted and cooled

40g/1½oz dark chocolate, melted

1 Preheat the oven to 200°C/400°F/gas mark 6. Line a large baking sheet with non-stick baking parchment.

2 Combine the plain flour, gram flour and semolina in a large mixing bowl. Add the baking powder, vanilla bean paste, cardamom seeds and icing sugar, then slowly pour in the melted butter, stirring until well combined. Use your hands to bring the mixture together into a dough.

3 Divide the cookie dough into 12 balls of equal size, then place them on the baking sheet, spacing them evenly apart.

4 Bake for 10–12 minutes, or until just starting to brown around the edges.

5 Remove from the oven and leave to cool on the baking sheet.

6 Once the cookies have fully cooled, drizzle over the melted chocolate and set aside until the chocolate has set.

Index

220

222

223

Acknowledgements

A huge thank you to everyone who was involved in the making of this book, particularly to my publisher, Fiona Robertson, and Emily Preece-Morrison, my project and copy editor. To Karen Smith for masterfully art directing the shoot and designing the book, and also to the larger editorial team, Kathy Steer and Vanessa Bird, for checking everything so diligently.

For the photography, thank you to Gareth Morgans for the wonderful food photographs. Thank you also to Bianca Nice, for her food styling, Charlotte Whatcott for assisting and to Hannah Wilkinson for sourcing (and sometimes making) such beautiful props.

Thanks to my fabulous food team, Sonali Shah and supertaster extraordinaire Andy Mountfield.

Thanks most to those who make my life evergreen: Zoltan, Mini Beans, Lala, Minmin, Nayan, Jaime, Fiondra, Eila, Honour, Willow, Atticus, Jill, Doo, Loodley, Steve.

Nisha Katona

224

MEAT FREE MOWGLI